NAUTILUS® FITNESS
FOR WOMEN
Michael D. Wolf, Ph.D.

Contemporary Books, Inc.
Chicago

Library of Congress Cataloging in Publication Data

Wolf, Michael D.
    Nautilus fitness for women.

    Includes index.
    1. Weight lifting.   2. Physical fitness for women.
3. Weight lifting—Equipment and supplies.   I. Title.
GV546.W64   1983   796.4'1'088042   83-10050
ISBN 0-8092-5491-3

Cover photograph by Ariel Skelley.

All Photos in Chapter 2 © Marti Cohen-Wolf
except where credited otherwise.

Illustrations for Chapters 4-7
by Vanessa Hill and Shelley Eshleman

Published by Contemporary Books, Inc.
180 North Michigan Avenue, Chicago, Illinois 60601
Manufactured in the United States of America
Library of Congress Catalog Card Number: 83-10050
International Standard Book Number: 0-8092-5491-3

Published simultaneously in Canada by
Beaverbooks, Ltd.
195 Allstate Parkway
Valleywood Business Park
Markham, Ontario L3R 4T8
Canada

CONTENTS

ACKNOWLEDGMENTS

A short list of thank-you's to some special people:

Nancy Crossman, my editor at Contemporary Books, for making it all happen;

Ed Farnham, General Manager of Nautilus Sports/Medical Industries, Inc., for everything;

My illustrators, *Vanessa Hill* and *Shelley Eshleman,* for doing a three month job in one month;

My cover photo crew, who did a knockout job on *very* short notice: photographer *Ariel Skelley,* stylist *Daphne White,* makeup/hair stylist *Bobbi Brown,* model *Nora Eichvalds;*

Dr. Murray Low for permission to shoot the book cover in the Westchester Cardiac Rehabilitation Center; Brenda Bernhardt Frasca and Major Steve Butcher, my flexible friends in Chapter 2; and

My wife *Marti,* who (with excuses to George Benson) is the star of my life story.

CHAPTER 1

INTRODUCTION

"I *know* these machines were just delivered and seem brand-new, but they look like medieval torture devices!" That's the reaction most women have to seeing a Nautilus machine for the first time. "Boy, they'll probably slap pounds of muscle on me at a time. Get me out of here!" That's the second reaction, and it's just as misguided as the first.

Whether you're a professional athlete or a 45-year-old housewife who can't tell a football from a baseball, Nautilus can have a strong impact on your life. Properly conducted Nautilus training, combined with good dietary habits, will do more to shape your body than any other form of exercise. You most likely will not grow larger muscles. You will, on the other hand, see almost miraculous shaping and toning from just about 60 minutes a week of hard exercise.

The Nautilus Fitness Book for Women is a step-by-step guide to total fitness through Nautilus, aerobic exercise, and nutrition. It is not a man's book that has four paragraphs devoted to women. It is expressly written to tell a woman everything she needs to know to use Nautilus to its maximum, which is not always easy considering that most of the machines are designed for men.

WHAT NAUTILUS CAN DO FOR YOU

What does the word *fitness* mean to you? Do you consider yourself fit? Does the fact that you haven't seen a doctor in years qualify you as fit?

Perhaps the best definition is that attributed to Dr. Richard Keelor, of the President's Council on Physical Fitness:

> Physical fitness really implies more than the ability to do a day's work without running out of gas, or surviving the emergency of snow shovelling or grass cutting. It is also a state of well-being that breeds confidence, poise, posture, physical ability, and an exhilarating feeling of buoyancy.

What it all adds up to is a fuller enjoyment of life. And Nautilus has become an important part of the process for tens of thousands of women from all walks of life.

What kinds of women train on Nautilus equipment? Just before I wrote this chapter I took a quick tour of the fitness center. I saw about 20 women there, ranging in age from 15 to 72. Their ranks included:

- an Olympic gold medalist in swimming (Wendy Boglioli, 1976, 4 × 100 freestyle relay, Montreal), now an executive, wife, and mother;
- eight housewives squeezing workouts in "before the kids get home from school";
- a medical illustrator/runner on her "lunch" break;
- twin 15-year-old sisters who gave their unconvinced mother a membership for Christmas;
- their mother, now a convert;
- two grandmothers in their 60s who can outexercise Jane Fonda.

As part of a total fitness program of strength training, aerobic exercise, and nutrition, Nautilus has something to offer everyone. And because you're a woman, with unique body chemistry, you can get all the benefits that men get *without* growing big muscles. How's that for an offer you can't refuse?

"You mean those monstrous machines won't turn me into a bodybuilder or a bearded lady?" That's what I said. If you're among the 95 percent of all women with 30 times less male sex hormone flowing through their veins than the average man, you just won't be able to grow big muscles. You will,

Strength, endurance, and power can be beautiful in a woman. (Photo courtesy of University of Iowa Women's Athletics.)

thanks to the wonders of evolution or creation (I'm not taking a stand), be able to tone, or firm, or reshape any body part you wish and show the same "percent strength gain" that men will.

Research has shown that a man and a woman may both increase their strength by 50 percent over six months, but the woman will show only a fraction of the muscle growth that the man will.

Find a tape measure and check the girth of your upper arm, midway between the shoulder and elbow. That number—say 10 inches—may not change at all over the next six months, but if you're like the thousands of women training on Nautilus, it'll be 10 inches of smooth, sleek muscle the next time

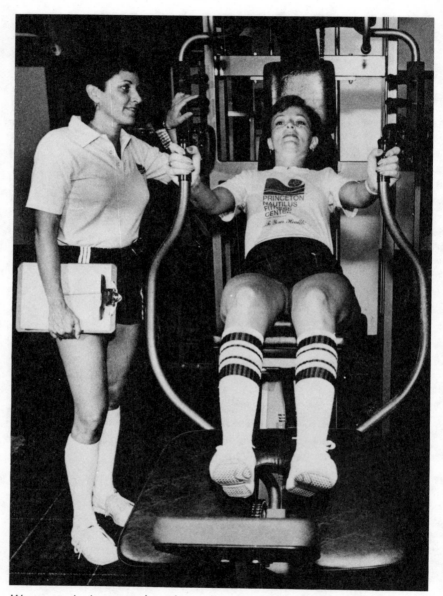

Women gain in strength without the major size increases that men see.
(Photo courtesy of Michaela McMillan.)

you measure it. That's the beauty of strength training for women!

Too bad Michelangelo didn't have Nautilus. The machines are really Space Age sculptor's tools. You can do calisthenics until you're blue in the face, but a Nautilus machine lets you focus on individual areas and reshape them with high-intensity exercise. Don't be scared off—*high intensity* doesn't mean "Call the ambulance and get the oxygen." It *does* mean that the 10 minutes of calisthenics that leaves you bored and asking, "Okay, what's next?" just isn't enough.

I'm not going to lie to you—a Nautilus workout is not the pleasure equivalent of two weeks in Hawaii. On the other hand, it will change your life so much that you'll beg for more. If you're a Wendy Boglioli, who rode hard swimming, great coaching (by husband Bernie, among others), and Nautilus to Olympic gold, we're talking about *high* intensity. If you're just out to do a little reshaping, however, the sacrifice and pain will be much easier to bear.

What happens, you ask, if muscles *do* start to appear in the "wrong" places? No big deal; all you have to do is decrease the intensity a bit. That will probably mean lifting lighter weights or training only twice a week. You are in control. You can sculpt your body any way you wish.

Don't forget about the many other nice changes you're going to see: a stronger and healthier heart, better lungs, improved control over body weight, increased ability to handle stress and tension, a delay in the aging process, improved mental function, and on and on.

DEFINING THE BENEFITS FURTHER

Expect to see physiological changes in three areas: strength, flexibility, and cardiovascular endurance. Don't be surprised if these change your entire life, though, because they add up to just one thing: improved self-image. Call it personal power, or self-worth, or self-actualization, or anything you want; you're going to feel an inner strength you haven't felt before. It's the one thread that runs through every woman's account of her Nautilus training experience.

The physical changes brought about by strength training help both athletes and housewives. (Photo courtesy of University of Iowa Women's Athletics.)

Strength Benefits

Strength is an integral but often unappreciated human faculty that affects your everyday life, whether you are an athlete or a nonathlete. Whether you're lifting the baby, the groceries, a 35-ounce softball bat, or a 12-pound bowling ball, strength makes it possible.

Research has clearly shown that women gain every bit as much, if not more, from strength training as do men in terms of strength gain. Since 20–30 times less testosterone circles in your veins than in men's veins, you rarely can gain the size that men do. All the benefits (strength) without the costs (bulging biceps)! An occasional woman has both an abnormally high testosterone level for her sex and the genetic ability to show hypertrophy (size gain). Though no one really knows how accurate this guess is, the experts figure that only between one and five out of every 100 women might fall into this category. If you don't want size, but you seem to be getting it from your training, you don't have an excuse to quit. Just reduce your intensity. End of problem!

The amount of strength gain you will see can only be guessed at, for every muscle responds differently to training. The untrained reader might triple her biceps strength but only double her triceps strength in the course of six months' training, working equally hard on the two muscles. My own lats and pectorals appear to grow at just the thought of strength work, but I never seem to be able to grow biceps!

The sky really is the limit on your potential gains. Expect to progress rapidly over the first few weeks, for your brain is very literally learning how to call on or "recruit" muscle for strength training exercises. Were you to measure strength on the first and 30th days of your first weightlifting month, you would see gains of 200 percent or more in nearly every exercise but only minor changes in muscle size. This is called the *neural component*. Actual muscular growth (see the last chapter) is called *hypertrophy*.

After the neural component of strength gains has run its course (within several weeks), results will establish themselves on a slow but relatively steady pace. Expect to hit plateaus, where you just seem to stop progressing, every once in a while. When you find yourself at this point, you have several choices, all of which we'll discuss later in detail. Briefly, they are: (1) try some eccentric or negative variations of the exercise; (2) find a different machine that works the plateaued muscle(s); or (3) give the muscle(s) a rest for several workouts.

Flexibility Benefits

The fact that this book contains a chapter on flexibility should already have told you something. Nautilus is not the sole answer to your flexibility needs. Several machines, most notably the Hip and Back machines, do a fine job and need not be augmented. Others don't fare as well.

Expect to see your flexibility at least maintained by Nautilus training. In many cases you'll see gains. *You will not become muscle-bound!*

Cardiovascular Benefits

The details are found in the last chapter, but Nautilus—while it gets your heart rate way up and keeps it there—is not more than 60 percent aerobic. You will be training the heart muscle, the breathing muscles, and a general and undefined metabolic ability to handle exercise stress. You will not, however, be performing an aerobic exercise or gaining aerobic benefits to the degree that swimming or running might offer them.

Since muscular strength plays a critical role in every aerobic sport, including 100-mile ultramarathons, Nautilus *will* im-

Nautilus played a key role in the training and rehabilitation of former world-class skier Ann Knudsen-Fitzpatrick. (Photo courtesy of Michaela McMillan.)

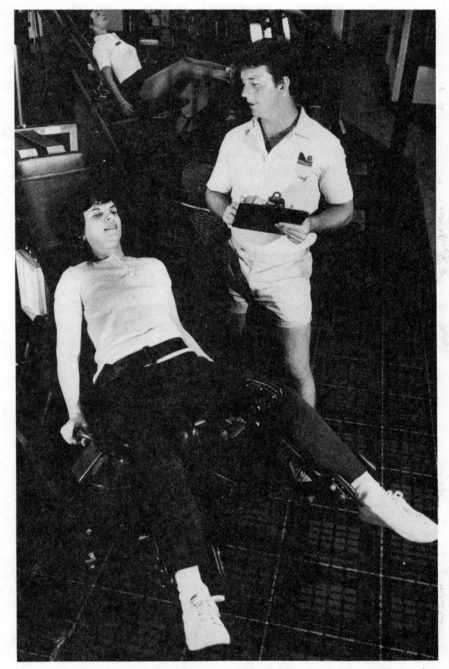

Proper supervision will allow you to reshape your body most effectively. (Photo courtesy of Michaela McMillan.)

prove performance in aerobic sports. It won't burn as many calories as proper aerobic exercise or raise your high-density lipoproteins (HDLs), the "good" form of cholesterol that appears to reduce the risk of coronary artery disease.

For total fitness the training effects of Nautilus must be combined with the aerobic benefits of activities such as swimming, running, cycling, and rowing. Chapter 9 is your complete guide to aerobics. A review of the remainder of the book's contents follows.

Chapter 2 is an illustrated guide to intelligent pre-Nautilus warm-up and stretching routines. Chapter 3 explains Nautilus training principles, the ones that apply to all Nautilus machines, in detail. Instructions for the use of 30 Nautilus machines, with emphasis placed on fitting women into equipment usually meant for men, are given in Chapters 4–7. In Chapter 8 are 10 Nautilus workouts plus suggestions on strength training for 16 different sports. As mentioned above, aerobic exercise is an important and necessary companion to Nautilus, and Chapter 9 contains everything you always wanted to know about the subject. Nutrition for the exercising woman (and her family) is discussed in Chapter 10, with loads of practical suggestions and advice. Chapter 11 answers the questions most commonly asked by exercising women, including those concerning pregnancy and exercise. Chapters 12 and 13 are intended for the curious. The book is concluded with detailed information on how Nautilus works on your body. Even if you're not ready for the nuts and bolts of it, this material should be interesting.

Don't stop now—read on to see what three brief workouts a week can do! But first review the following list, which will familiarize you with the location of the various muscles you'll be training.

YOUR MUSCLES: A GUIDE TO ANATOMICAL TERMS

Body Part	Anatomical Terms
Shoulders	Deltoids (in three parts: front, middle, rear)

Upper Arms	Biceps (front side) Triceps (rear side)
Forearms	Wrist Flexors (palm surface) Wrist Extensors (back surface)
Chest	Pectoralis Major
Upper Back	Latissimus Dorsi, Teres Major/Minor; Trapezius
Lower Back	Spinal Erectors
Hip Flexors	Iliopsoas, Rectus Femoris
Abdomen	Rectus Abdominus, Internal and External Obliques, Transverse Abdominus
Buttocks	Gluteus Maximus (or Hip Extensors)
Outside Buttocks	Gluteus Medius, Tensor Fascia Latae (Abductor Group)
Front Thigh	Quadriceps (in four parts: Vastus Medialis, Lateralis, and Intermedius; Rectus Femoris)
Back Thigh	Hamstrings (in three parts: Semitendinosus, Semimembranosus, Biceps Femoris)
Inside Thigh	Adductor Group
Calf	Gastrocnemius, Soleus
Shin	Tibialis Anterior

CHAPTER 2

GETTING STARTED: WARM-UP AND FLEXIBILITY

Some things just can't be rushed. While it's true that your *hard* strength training time can be limited to 60 minutes a week, you'll need to spend at least that much time on warm-ups and stretching.

You've probably been told that the first four reps on each machine are your warm-up and that your flexibility needs are met by the machines, which were designed to stretch you. Well, don't buy it. It's too quick, too dangerous, and too incomplete.

There are three main reasons why you need to start each workout with a warm-up and stretch. First, the medical/exercise science world has come to realize that sudden strenuous exercise, or *SSE* as it is known, can create major disturbances in heart function. Research has clearly shown that as little as a five-minute stationary bike warm-up can almost completely eliminate the dangers associated with SSE.

Second, permanent gains in flexibility, which are needed for everyday living as well as for athletic endeavors, occur only when the so-called "plastic element" of connective tissue is stretched and held for at least 20 seconds. Ballistic, or bouncing, stretches don't work because they stretch only the "elastic element." They have no effect on the more important plastic component. What's worse, they can do serious damage to it.

Finally, the plastic element can be stretched only if it has been warmed several degrees above resting temperature. Even if a machine *were* to hold you in a stretched position for

20 seconds, little would be achieved unless the tissue were warm enough to allow permanent plastic element stretch. Flexibility work *must* be preceded by at least a five-minute overall warm-up. No doubt you were taught that the warm-up should come second, but this is wrong. Warm-up first, then stretch.

What to do and for how long? Low-trauma, whole-body warm-ups are best. A brisk walk is excellent. Easy jumping jacks, rowing (if a rowing machine is available), jumping rope, or jogging on a minitrampoline will do the job. Avoid any exercises that apply too much force too quickly. A slow jog is acceptable; running isn't. Spend 5–10 minutes on the warm-up, and you can step up the pace gradually during that period.

What follows is a safe and effective flexibility program that should precede your Nautilus work. Nineteen stretches are shown and described; select at least one from each category and spend at least 45 seconds on each one. This should take 10–15 minutes.

Following your 20- to 30-minute Nautilus work, spend some time warming down. If you have the time to spare, another run through the stretching program would add significantly more to permanent flexibility gain. At the very least, devote five minutes to one of the whole-body warm-ups. Believe me, it will make a difference.

A Selection of Warm-Ups

Body Area	Choose from These Stretches
Neck	Lateral Flexion
	Lateral Rotation
Torso	Side Bends
Upper Back	Meditation Sit
Rear Shoulder	Rear Deltoid Stretch
	Behind-Neck Stretch
Front Shoulder	Iron Cross
	Hands behind Back

Wrist	Wrist Extension
Low Back	Lying Knees to Chest
	Lying One Knee to Chest
Abdominals	Half-Cobra Stretch
Quadriceps	Standing Quad Stretch
	Prone Quad Stretch
	Kneeling Quad Stretch
Hip Extensors	Lying One Knee to Chest
Hamstrings	Lying One Knee to Chest
	Half-Lotus Hamstring Stretch
Groin	Lotus
Overall	Multi-Stretch
	Sit and Twist

(**Below, left**) *LATERAL FLEXION: Grasp one elbow and pull gently while tilting the head in a right-to-left plane to the other side.* (**Below, right**) *LATERAL ROTATION: Place one hand on the other shoulder while rotating the head in the opposite direction.*

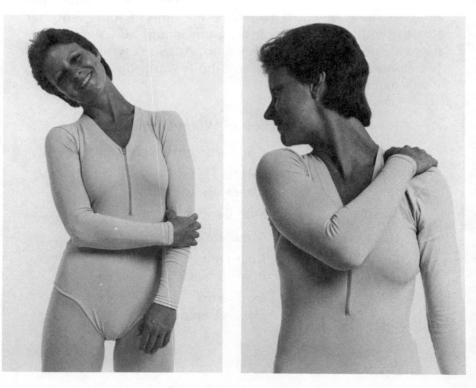

(Left) *SIDE BENDS: Bend in a right-to-left plane, keeping the hands by the sides. Keep the stomach tucked in and the back flat.* (Below) *MEDITATION SIT: Cross your arms over the knees and gently stretch the upper back.*

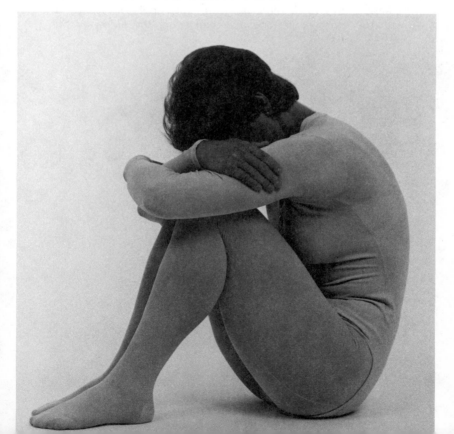

(Above) *REAR DELTOID STRETCH: Pull one arm across the chest with the other to stretch the back of the shoulder.* **(Below)** *BEHIND-NECK STRETCH: Raise both arms behind the head. Pull one elbow across the midline with the other hand. You may pull either the elbow or the wrist.*

(**Left**) *IRON CROSS: Raise both arms to the sides and draw back as far as possible. Minimize back arching.* (**Below**) *HANDS BEHIND BACK: Cross the fingers behind the back and gently lift the arms to stretch the front shoulders. Avoid back arching.*

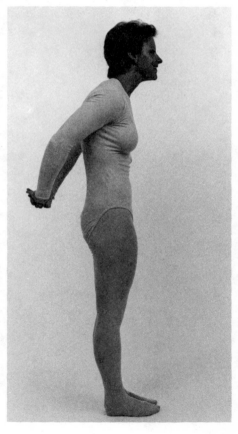

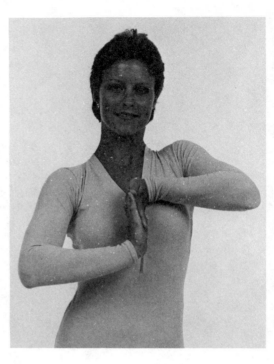

WRIST EXTENSION:
Invert the hands and
gently stretch
backward.

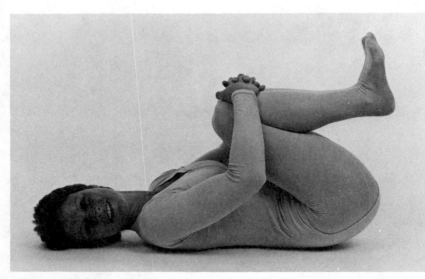

LYING KNEES TO CHEST: Bring both knees to the chest and pull gently.

(Above) *HALF-COBRA
STRETCH: From a prone
position, leave the forearms on
the floor and gently lift up,
stretching the abdominals.*
(Right) *STANDING QUAD
STRETCH: Stabilizing against a
wall or chair, grasp one ankle
and pull back toward the
buttocks. Keep the knees
together. Minimize arching of
the back.*

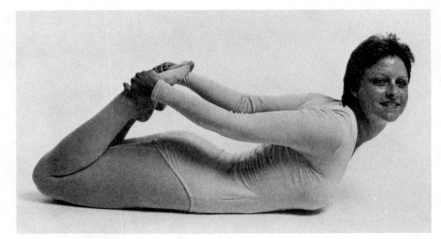

(Above) *PRONE QUAD STRETCH: From a prone position, reach back and grasp the ankles. Pull gently back to the buttocks.* **(Below)** *KNEELING QUAD STRETCH: With a pad under the knee that is down, grasp the ankle and gently pull back to the buttocks. Minimize back arching.*

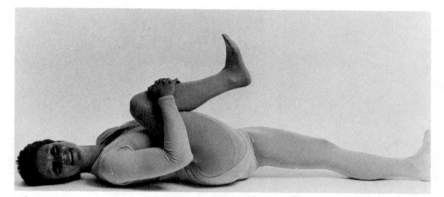

(**Above**) *LYING ONE KNEE TO CHEST: Proceed as in Lying Knees to Chest, but stretch one leg/hip at a time.* (**Below**) *HALF-LOTUS HAMSTRING STRETCH: Sit forward with back totally straight and head up. Grasp and hold at the first point where you feel the stretch in the hamstrings. Pressing forward with the chest helps maintain correct back position. This may be done with both legs extended out front.*

LOTUS: Keeping the knees close to the floor, gradually bring the heels in toward the groin area.

(Above) MULTISTRETCH: Lean forward, again with a perfectly straight back and with the head up, and cross the arms to the opposite knees. Keep the ankles flexed toward you to stretch the calves as well. (Below) SIT AND TWIST: Sit with the back straight, legs extended, and toes pointed back toward the torso. Bend one knee and place the foot on the outside of the other knee. Turn toward the leg with the bent knee. Try to keep the shoulders as level as possible.

CHAPTER 3

TIME-EFFICIENT FITNESS: NAUTILUS PHILOSOPHY AND TRAINING PRINCIPLES

Nautilus is more than a form of strength training. It is, above all else, a philosophy. The machines are nothing but tools for the achievement of high-intensity training in short periods of time. Embracing Nautilus means accepting three simple words–go *to failure*.

This chapter presents Nautilus training philosophy and principles. For the most part, they can be applied to any form of strength training. One of the truths about Nautilus is that the machines were designed to apply the philosophy; the machines *didn't* come first. Not all manufacturers can make that claim!

INTENSITY AND ISOLATION

The two cornerstones of strength training are intensity and isolation. Indeed, the two go hand in hand. Without isolation, it is impossible to achieve sufficient intensity to stimulate maximal training gains. Strength work must be brief and intense. One set, taken to the point of momentary muscular failure, makes a maximal demand on the system for strength gain.

Arthur Jones, founder of the Nautilus system, has been quoted as stating, "It took me 20 years to learn that two sets are better than four and another 20 to learn that one set was better than two." The bottom line is that if intensity is great enough, and if the muscle is taken to the point where it is no longer capable of contraction (momentary muscular failure), one set will induce maximal strength gains but will have a minimal destructive effect on the individual's structural integrity and energy reserves. An added bonus of this approach is that recovery is more rapid than usual, leaving an unexpectedly high capacity for other pursuits.

Consider pursuits like golf. Ken Hutchins, of Nautilus Florida, put me through a brutal 11-machine, 19-minute workout for the benefit of some visitors one day. Ken is not known for the quality of mercy, by the way. True to form, he left me on the showroom floor in a semiconscious state. Ninety minutes later I teed off on our local golf course and proceeded to shoot a two-over 38 on the front nine, then my lowest nine ever. Rapid strength gains *plus* the ability to live a normal life after the weight room? Not bad stuff, this Nautilus.

What about isolation? Why not dream up devices that work many muscles at the same time in the interest of reducing training time even further? The answer is that muscles are nothing more than unintelligent machines, doing whatever the brain asks of them. The goal in strength training should most logically be to take each muscle, isolate it, and develop its cellular, structural ability to contract as well and as quickly as possible. With this background, the muscles are taken out into the real world, or onto the athletic field, where the brain learns to use them in perfectly skill-specific ways. Train the triceps carefully and specifically, in isolation, then train the brain to use them for shooting basketballs, throwing softballs, or hitting golf balls.

Nautilus machines are designed to isolate muscles wherever possible. In many instances the machines eliminate the problem of weak links in the chain so that large muscles can be stimulated directly, not worked through other, smaller muscles. Take for an example the Nautilus Pullover machine. The latissimus dorsi muscles of the back, which attach to the upper arm near the shoulder, are almost directly stressed through your performance of the exercise with your elbows. Were you to attempt to train your lats with an old, pulley-type pulldown bar, you'd find that your elbow flexors (biceps and brachialis) and forearms would be sharing the load with

The Nautilus Pullover machine allows relative isolation of the latissimus dorsi of the upper back. (Photo by Michael D. Wolf)

the lats. Not only does this reduce the intensity on the lats; it also means that should these weaker links fail, the exercise ends before the lats reach momentary muscular failure.

How Do You Quantify Intensity?

As soon as you learn the machines, there's only one level of intensity to worry about: 100 percent. Strength training must be brief and intense. It *cannot* be long and intense. You'll find that as your workouts get longer your intensity starts to decline noticeably.

Doesn't it make sense to give 20 minutes of 100 percent a try first? One of the many quotable quotes of Arthur Jones addresses the time and intensity question: "Instead of seeing how *long* we can make our athletes train to gain strength, we should be trying to see how *little* they can train to get the same results." It seems to me that if you find 20 minutes insufficient, you can easily add an exercise or two or try an

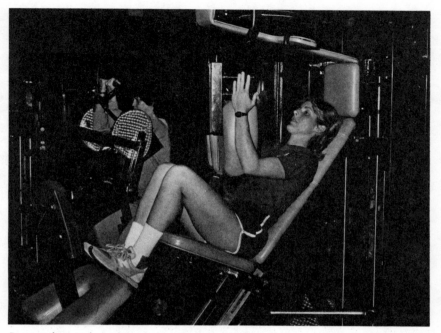

Proper form plus 100 percent intensity is a near guarantee of good results. (Photo by Michael D. Wolf)

extra set here and there. Perhaps optimum training time for you is 29 minutes, or 38 minutes. We really don't know how to tell yet. It doesn't make sense, though, to do three sets of 18 exercises over 90 minutes and then try to figure out where to cut back. Tens of thousands of athletes and plain people off the street have found brief, high-intensity work sufficient. *Brief* means 30 minutes or less; *high intensity* means 100 percent.

My favorite summary phrase on the issue of intensity and workout duration is "More is not better." This is about the hardest training habit to break and probably the worst to keep. Give 20–30 minutes of 100 percent a try.

TRAINING FREQUENCY

If you're into "more is better," you're not going to like this. The *maximum* you'll want to train is three times a week, and that doesn't mean Monday, Tuesday, and Wednesday. Workouts must be followed by at least 48 hours of rest, and many of you may need more than that.

The two guidelines to follow here are (1) your results and (2) your energy level outside the fitness center. Three 30-minute workouts at 100 percent can be too many. If you see a drop in energy level, or results are slow in coming, try cutting back to highest-intensity work on Mondays and Fridays, with 80 percent workouts in between. Fight the urge to train longer, or more frequently, if you're not gaining as quickly as you or the staff personnel expect. Once again, try shorter routines first. If they work, fine. If they don't, you can begin to spend more time training.

THE MATTER OF TECHNIQUE AND SUPERVISION

Let's face it: one of the major reasons that people are purchasing this book is the frequent lack of expertise among fitness center personnel. This lack is understandable because too many entrepreneurs pay too little attention to staff education.

This book was written to be the ultimate Nautilus instruction manual. A five-sentence set of instructions may look good on paper, but it fails when you climb into your first machine. Women have received a particularly raw deal, usually getting a paragraph or two in the opening chapters. The proper use of Nautilus equipment demands detailed instructions.

Don't be afraid to take this book with you to the machines. Find a slow hour at your fitness center, find a good instructor, and take some time to learn the ropes.

How can you identify a good instructor? I met and taught hundreds of Nautilus trainers in the time I spent at headquarters in Florida. If your local instructors spent time in Lake Helen, chances are good that they know more about Nautilus than the average Joe. Similarly, there has been a move by Nautilus Florida to send some educational seminars on the road. This has helped reach many who couldn't make the trip to Florida. Finally, while schooling is far from a guarantee, look at your instructors' educational credentials. A bachelor's degree in physical education should be the minimum. A master's degree in exercise physiology gets a gold star.

THE LUCKY 14—NAUTILUS TRAINING PRINCIPLES

1. Perform only one set of four to six exercises for the lower body and six to eight exercises for the upper body. This may vary if you have a sport interest such as running or field hockey. Perform no more than 12 exercises in a workout. Each exercise on a Nautilus compound machine counts as one exercise. That is, if

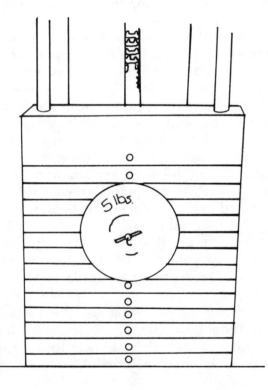

Weight loads can be increased in small increments by pinning one- to 7½-pound weights to the stack.

you perform both the Lateral Raise and the Overhead Press on the Double Shoulder machine, you've used one machine but done two exercises.

2. Select a very easy resistance on each exercise that allows you to complete 8–12 repetitions for the upper body and 12–15 reps for the lower body. Your first few workouts should be very easy to do, using light weights.

3. Continue each exercise to the point of momentary muscular failure, i.e., where no further repetitions can be performed in good form. When you've reached the point where you discard technique just to get out another rep, you're finished. When your target number of reps has been reached, increase the weight load about 5 percent during the next workout.

4. To get the best results in the least amount of time, remember the phrase *touch and go*. It refers to the completion of each single repetition, when your chosen weight load briefly touches down on the weight stack. *Touch and go* tells you to pause only momentarily between repetitions. Resting will not necessarily reduce your results, but it will lengthen your workout.

5. Always work the large muscles first and move to progressively smaller muscles. This serves to avert general fatigue before the more important, major muscles have been trained. The sequence in which the machines are presented in the instructional chapters that follow is the order you should follow.

6. Concentrate on flexibility by slowly letting the machines draw you into the stretched position. Don't use the machines to pull you to places you've never been before.

7. Accentuate the lowering, or the negative phase, of every repetition. The advice you've probably heard to raise for two seconds and lower for four is nonsensical, for there is about a threefold difference in range of contraction among machines. A two-second positive contraction on some machines will be fast; on others it may be slow. Your guideline? Lift the weights so that

they move slowly and never jerk or accelerate. Lower the weight stack at about half that speed.

8. Move slower, not faster, if ever in doubt about speed of movement. A good trick is to watch the weight stack, if possible, at the top of its ascent. If you move at the correct speed, the stack will reach a position and hold it without bouncing.

9. If strength gains are to be maximized, and cardiovascular gains minimized, you may rest between machines. If you'd like to maximize the latter, move as rapidly as possible between machines. If you can work out during slack time, have a partner ready to set seat heights and weights to speed things along even further.

10. Do everything possible to isolate and work each muscle or muscle group to exhaustion.

11. Constantly attempt to increase the number of repetitions (to the target number) or the amount of weight, or both. *Do not* sacrifice form in an attempt to produce results. If you reach a plateau at a particular weight, lower the weight, try a different machine that works the same muscle, or just give the muscle a rest for a few workouts. Expect plateaus once in a while; we all reach them. Negatives may help here.

12. Train no more than three times a week. As discussed above, you should leave at least 48 hours between workouts. If you find yourself fatigued, or progressing more slowly than expected, cut back.

13. *Keep accurate records.* Seat height should be set and recorded during your first workout. Each day, make sure to note the date, number of reps, weight load, and any variations such as negative-only exercise.

14. Vary the workouts often. Chapter 8 offers a number of suggested workouts, as well as some sport-specific training ideas.

CHAPTER 4

THE LOWER BODY

The next four chapters will guide you through the use of thirty different Nautilus machines or exercises. They are presented in their order of use, i.e., lower body, torso, arms, and neck.

You will be pleasantly surprised at how easily your legs can be reshaped through lower body Nautilus training and calorie control. Remember that strength training can either tone (firm) or add muscle mass, but that fat *reduction* comes only through caloric deficit—burning more than you take in.

Don't be discouraged if you find the first two Nautilus machines the most difficult to learn—they are well worth the effort!

THE DUO HIP AND BACK MACHINE
Primary muscles worked: gluteus maximus, hamstrings,
erector spinae group

1. Set the pin carefully at a weight established by fitness center personnel.
2. Separate the two movement arms and enter from the front or side, placing one leg over the top roller, the other over the bottom roller.
3. Centering your body (in a right-to-left direction), grasp the handles lightly and position yourself so that the axis of hip rotation matches the axis of cam rotation. For many people, the hips will be positioned correctly at the machine axis when their arms are fully extended,

but this is not the determining factor. (Don't let anyone tell you that it is.) Strive to keep your hip axis at the machine axis.

4. Fasten the safety belt snugly around the waist.
5. Perform several scissorlike movements with the legs, *without* lifting the weight stack. Start these alternating scissors with small amplitude movements, then progress to full-range flexion (knee to chest) and extension (knee away from chest). These will serve as a brief but effective warm-up and will ensure that both you and the machine are in working order.
6. With one leg in a fully extended position, bring the opposite leg to a fully flexed position. Slowly bring the flexed leg down to meet the extended leg. *Do not* straighten the upper or flexed leg toward the ceiling as it extends. *Hold the extended leg perfectly steady.* Let the ankle on the extending leg gradually flex so that the toes point downward.
7. You're now ready to go. With both legs extended fully and the toes pointed, squeeze and isometrically hold the position for at least two seconds. While you may get a greater range of motion if you arch your back at this point, the orthopedic risks outweigh the fitness benefits. *Don't arch.*
8. While holding the leg that just extended perfectly steady (you can watch the cam or the chain behind your head), let the other leg very slowly flex back toward the chest. Get a maximum stretch here to allow the fullest possible range of contraction for the hamstrings and gluteal group.
9. Holding the leg that is down steady (not easy), bring the flexed leg down as described above (steps 6 and 7). Repeat.
10. When you reach momentary muscular failure, defined as the inability to maintain perfect form while exercising, or when you feel the *slightest* bit of unusual pain, immediately bring the extended or down leg up. This will lower the weight stack most efficiently.

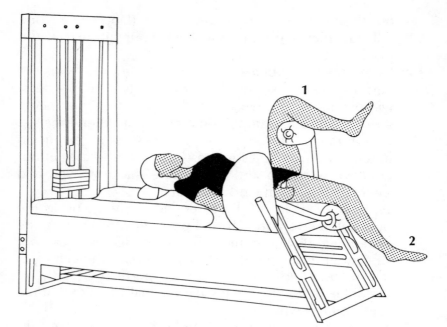

Hip and Back, starting position.
1. Do not straighten this leg toward the ceiling!
2. Keep this leg totally motionless.

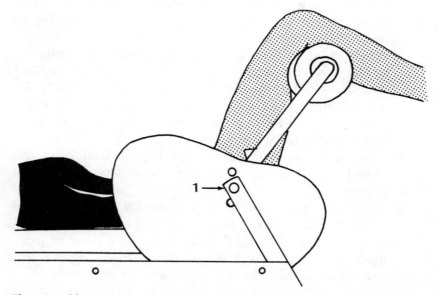

The axis of hip movement must match the axis of cam rotation.

THE DUO-SQUAT MACHINE

Primary muscles worked: gluteus maximus, hamstrings,
quadriceps, gastrocnemius/soleus
(calf)

1. Before entering the machine, locate the seat adjustment lever on the lower right side. Pull up on this
handle and move the seat as far from the weight stack
as possible.
2. Sit on the seat and place your shoulders under the two
pads, with your feet on the machine base in front of the
seat. *Make sure the seat is locked into position* by
pushing backward against any vertical part of the machine frame.
3. Seat adjustment: Using that lower right seat adjustment
handle, slowly inch yourself forward toward the weight
stack. You have reached the proper position, which
allows full-range, correct, variable-resistance exercise,
when these three things happen:
    a. the movement arms touch the bolts extending out of
    the crossbar several degrees of rotation *before your
    knees lock out;*
    b. the chain completely unwinds off the cam on flexion
    toward the torso; and
    c. your knee flexes almost back to your chest.
    *This seat position, which should be recorded for poster-
    ity like all others, should be established only with
    trained personnel present.*
4. Double-check that the seat is firmly in position by again
pushing back on any vertical part of the machine frame.
5. Extend one leg to the point where the movement arm
reaches the crossbar. You should not be able to lock
your knee at this point. Locking can cause serious
damage to the supporting ligaments behind the knee.
Experienced users report that the compressive forces
on the neck and shoulders are reduced greatly if you
set the seat as described here.
6. Straighten the other leg to meet the first. Keep your
hands on the handles with a loose grip, your shoulders
firmly in the pads, and your head back.

Duo-Squat, starting position.
1. Do not allow this knee to drop and lock.
2. Go for a full but pain-free flexion here.
3. Keep the head back and shoulders firmly in the pads.

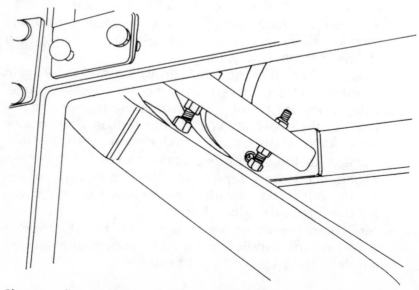

Close-up of movement arms against crossbar bolts.

7. Holding one leg extended, let the other leg flex as far back toward the torso as possible. Pause and hold here briefly, then extend the leg slowly to meet the other leg.
8. Repeat with the second leg and continue alternating to the point of momentary muscular failure or any abnormal pain.

Akinetic/Infimetric Attachment

Some Duo-Squats are equipped with an Akinetic/Infimetric bar that swings from the left weight stack guide rod around to a position between the two chains.

Infimetric exercise is a unique form of movement in which the opposing limbs (here the right and left legs) are played off against each other. Very simply, one leg (or arm) pulls or pushes while the other limb resists. Without an intervening stack of weights, you can achieve an intense positive and negative workout. This results from the combination of concentric contraction (one leg extending or contracting in a "positive" manner) and eccentric contraction (the other leg forcefully resisting extension or contracting in a "negative" fashion). Throw a weight stack between the two limbs and you've got exquisite muscular agony known as akinetic work.

Remembering that we're after quality, not quantity, and that quality means intensity, you should give infimetric and akinetic exercise a try, but only after you've learned the machine and have been using Nautilus for at least two months. Ask your instructors for help.

Instructions for Akinetic Duo-Squat:
1. Use the same seat and body positions that were detailed above.
2. Before beginning the exercise, swing the restraining bar into position so that it is squarely above the center of the weight stack. Its task is to prevent the stack from getting closer to the crosspiece above it.
3. Extend one leg to the final extension position (at the bolt on the crosspiece), then extend the other leg to

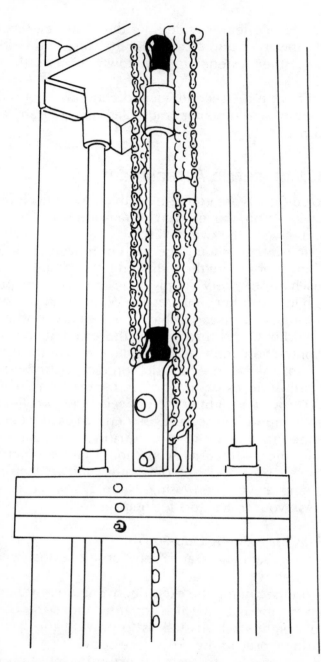

Close-up of the infimetric bar in position above the stack.

raise the weight stack to the restraining bar. Your weight setting will and should be lower than usual. No research has been done to tell us how much lower or how many reps are needed. Shoot for a weight that will allow 15–20 reps (one leg extension being one rep). This will mean about a 50 percent reduction in weight load, but it varies.

4. At the point where the weight stack meets the restraining bar you will begin the exercise by extending the second leg as forcefully as possible while resisting it with the fully extended opposite leg. Concentrate on working through the full range of motion and *do not* let the weight stack drop off the restraining bar. If it does so before you've reached 15 reps, decrease the weight during the next session. *Work slowly.*

Instructions for Infimetric Duo-Squat:

1. The only difference between akinetic and infimetric is that your legs will be supporting only one weight plate in infimetric work. Akinetic exercise requires that you add measurably to the leg-against-leg battle with several weight plates.

2. To work infimetrically, pull the pin out of the weight stack and follow all instructions as detailed for akinetics.

THE LEG EXTENSION MACHINE (SUPER, FIXED SEAT, COMPOUND LEG VERSIONS)

Primary muscles worked: quadriceps (and hip extensors when performing leg squat on Compound Leg)

You may encounter three variations of this machine. The first does not have an adjustable seat back. The second is identical but for the inclusion of the adjustable seat. The third, the Compound Leg machine, is an imposing device that pairs a Leg Press attachment with an adjustable-seat Leg Extension unit.

1. If the seat back is *not* adjustable, go scout out a few upholstered pads to shimmy you forward. If your center does not have any, ask them to get some. If you don't get your pads, get your money back.

2. Sit forward on the seat and place your feet behind the roller pads. Scoot backward until the backs of your knees are touching the front of the seat. If this places your knee axis (try to picture one) behind the machine's axis of rotation, scoot forward to match them.

3. Without the adjustable seat feature, place sufficient pads behind you to fill the space between your back, when your knee is in position, and the seat back. These pads should run the length of your back. Small women may need two pads. If you can get only short pads, you may put one on top of the other and hold them in place with your back.

4. If your seat is adjustable, lift up the adjustment lever and move the seat back to meet your back. The criterion for body position is, once again, knee alignment. With the seat set, recheck knee position. Fasten the safety belt.

5. Keeping your head and shoulders relaxed and against the seat back, and your hands in a loose grip, straighten both legs slowly from the fully stretched or flexed position (heels back towards buttocks) to full extension. Hold this contraction for one full second, then lower at an even slower rate than you used to raise the weight.

6. Remember the words *touch and go.* In several exercises, including this one, you may be presented with the tempting opportunity to rest your weights on the weight stack between reps. *Don't even think about it! Touch and go* means the most you are allowed to do is touch the weight stack down, then go. This is time-efficient fitness, so if you can get the intensity up, you can get the time down.

7. Continue with full extensions, brief holds, and full flexions until momentary muscular failure.

Compound Leg Machine

If you have access to a Compound Leg machine, you won't

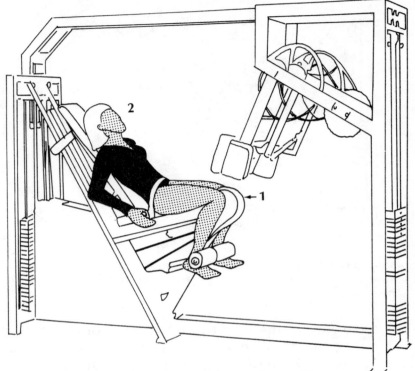

Compound Leg, Knee Extension exercise, starting position.
1. Keep the knee axis at the cam axis.
2. Keep the head and shoulders back and relaxed.

need to use the Duo-Squat. While the Duo-Squat offers some definite advantages over the Compound Leg's Leg Press, you don't need to do both. In fact, the rapid switch to Leg Press after Leg Extension, based on the Preexhaustion principle (see Chapter 12 for details), makes this perhaps the most intense station on your Nautilus circuit. It definitely gets my vote.

8. *With all possible speed,* sit up and pull the adjustable seat forward as far as possible.
9. Flip down the Leg Press foot pads into their locked position.
10. Place your feet on the pads with your toes turned slightly inward. With the seat this far forward, you will be *very* balled up behind the Leg Press foot pads. This

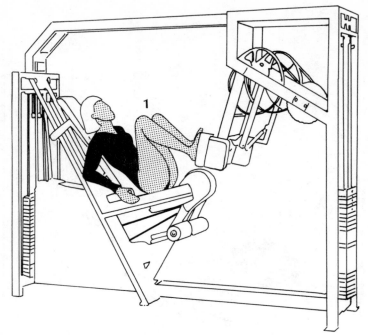

Compound Leg, Leg Press exercise, starting position.
1. *Move the seat back forward to get a full but pain-free flexion at the knee.*

serves to get the fullest possible range of contraction out of the hip extensors and quadriceps. *If this high degree of hip flexion causes any knee pain, cease immediately.* If reducing this angle by moving the seat back doesn't eliminate the pain, leave this exercise out of your workout!

11. Straighten both legs slowly to within a few inches of knee lock. Do not let your knees drop into a lock. Hold this position for at least one full second.

12. Allow as full a return stretch as possible, then repeat to momentary muscular failure.

13. Points to remember: Breathe normally, avoid head and neck tension, do not grip tightly, and stop at the first sign of any abnormal pain.

THE LEG CURL MACHINE
Primary muscles worked: hamstrings

1. Lie facedown on the machine. Have a spotter help you position yourself so that your knee axis is aligned with the machine's axis of rotation.

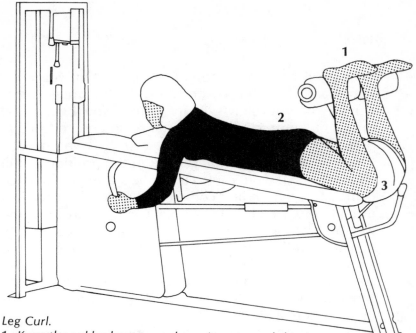

Leg Curl.
1. *Keep the ankles bent toward you (toes toward shins).*
2. *Keep the hips flat on the pad.*
3. *Keep the knee axis at the cam axis.*

2. Many women need an auxiliary pad under their bodies to elevate them into proper position. Again, if your center doesn't have one, ask for it. Get some friends together and let management know you're there! Nautilus of Virginia manufactures these pads to fit the Leg Curl machine perfectly.
3. Place your feet under the rollers only if you can do so comfortably. Some women find it difficult to thread their way underneath. If you're in this group, have a spotter lift the rollers for you by hand to ease entry.
4. Grasp handles either lightly or by hooking your wrists around them. Keep your head relaxed. You may let it extend up to watch the weight stack.
5. Curl your legs up slowly, keeping your ankles flexed so that your toes point toward your shins and always keeping your pelvis firmly planted on the machine. I know you've been told for years to let your buttocks rise and your back arch to get a fuller range of motion. This is another case of orthopedic risk (from compression of the spinal disks through back arching) outweighing one possible exercise benefit.

You will find, much to your surprise, that you get a significantly greater contraction of the upper hamstrings with your pelvis down. In time you'll get a nice range of contraction with a more intense effort. *Be prepared to use less weight than you think you need.*

6. Pause for at least one full second in the position of full contraction. If you can't clearly see the weight stack come to a smooth and complete stop, you've probably thrown the weights. In simple English, throwing the weights by moving too fast throws the benefits away.

7. Return to full leg extension, or wherever the pain-free limit might be. Healthy legs should have no trouble assuming this 180-degree position. If you find that you can rest the weights on the stack in this position, remember touch and go.

8. Repeat flexion and extension to momentary muscular failure.

THE HIP ADDUCTION MACHINE

Primary muscles worked: inner thigh adductors (bring legs together)

1. Standing alongside the machine, familiarize yourself with the adjustment mechanism. Pushing the lever in and turning will either separate the movement arms or move them closer together.

2. Sit in the machine and place the knees and ankles against their respective pads. You may need full-length pads behind your back to move you far enough forward. The middle of the knee should meet the middle of the knee pad.

3. Fasten the safety belt.

4. Use the adjustment lever to separate the legs as far as is comfortable.

5. Keeping the head and shoulders back and relaxed, contract the adductors smoothly and slowly, bringing the legs together. Use your knees to move the weight. Your ankles are only along for the ride. You may point your toes slightly inward.

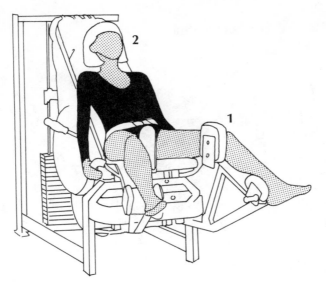

Hip Adductor.
1. *Exert all pressure by rolling the knees inward.*
2. *Keep the head and shoulders back and relaxed.*

6. At the completion of the contraction, squeeze the pads together and hold the position for a full second.
7. Return slowly to full abduction (stretch) and repeat to momentary muscular failure.

THE HIP ABDUCTION MACHINE
Primary muscles worked: gluteus medius, tensor fascia latae

1. Sit in the machine and place your legs in position. The knee pads should be at or slightly above knee level. Use full-length back pads if you find the pads too low on your leg.
2. Fasten the safety belt.
3. Keep your head and shoulders back and relaxed, your hand grip open and relaxed.
4. Abduct (spread) the legs as widely as possible but do it slowly. There is a great temptation here to throw the legs apart. *Don't.*
5. While abducting the legs, feel the pressure in the knee area, *not* the ankle area. You may visualize rolling the legs outward as they separate. This will help isolate the abductors.

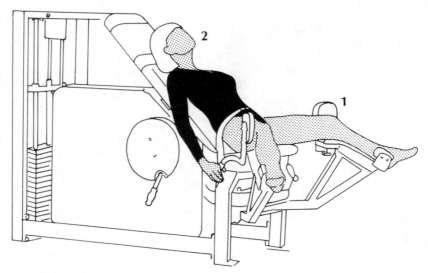

Hip Abductor.
1. Exert pressure by rolling the knees outward.
2. Shoulders back and relaxed!

6. Pause in the fully contracted (abducted) position for a full second, then return slowly. Touch and go, and repeat to momentary muscular failure.

THE COMBINATION HIP ADDUCTION-ABDUCTION MACHINE

Follow the instructions as detailed for the Hip Adduction and Hip Abduction machines above. Try adduction before abduction.

THE MULTIEXERCISE MACHINE CALF RAISE
Primary muscles worked: gastrocnemius, soleus

1. While you may feel more comfortable performing this exercise in bare or stockinged feet, that will increase the risk of damage to the small muscles of the foot. Keep your shoes on!
2. Find the padded waist belt and snap it onto the movement arm. Twist the belt once or twice to reduce its circumference. Small-waisted readers may need to twist the belt three or more times to get a snug fit.

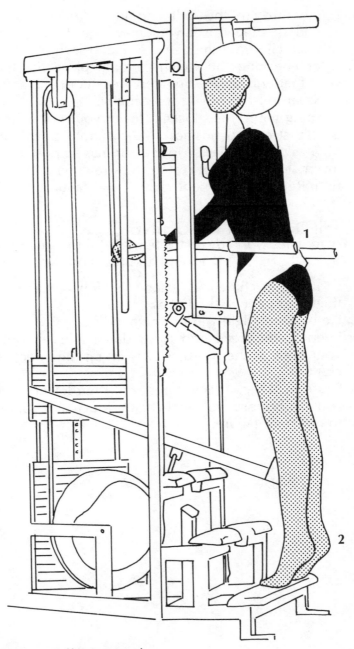

Multiexercise, Calf Raise exercise.
1. Make sure the belt is firmly in place above hips.
2. Get a full range of motion at the ankle.

3. Climb through the belt and lift it to waist level. It should sit snugly over your pelvic girdle. Don't begin this exercise until the belt is safe and secure.
4. After checking the weight setting, place the balls of your feet *only* on the first step. Reach out and grasp the crossbar in front of you for stability.
5. Keeping your knees locked, lower your body slowly to a fully stretched position. Now elevate slowly and as high as possible. Pause in the contracted position, then lower slowly. Do not rest in the stretched (down) position. Repeat to momentary muscular failure.

THE HIP FLEXOR MACHINE
Primary muscles worked: rectus femoris (of the quadriceps group) and the iliopsoas (or psoas)

1. Sit in the machine and fasten the safety belt across your thighs, just above the knees.
2. Lie back and lightly grasp the handles.
3. Keeping the head and torso down and relaxed, flex your body at the hip by slowly lifting the knees to the chest.
4. Pause in the contracted position, then lower slowly. If you can bottom the weight stack, touch and go. Repeat to muscular failure.

Hip Flexor.
1. Fasten the belt on the lower thighs.
2. Keep the head and shoulders back and relaxed.

CHAPTER 5

THE TORSO

Here are the machines that will reshape your torso. Your sleek new shape will be a result of waist-whittling (with the help of calorie control) and upper torso firming/building. Many women find that hard work on the pullover, chest, and shoulder machines gives them a moderate and pleasing V-shape. Feel free to select whichever torso machines you and your instructor think most important for *your* reshaping program.

THE PULLOVER MACHINE (Super Pullover, Pullover/Torso Arm Combination, Women's Pullover)
Primary muscles worked: latissimus dorsi, teres major/minor

The Super Pullover, which we can truthfully call the Men's Pullover, may just be too big for women. Nautilus finally introduced a women's version, which is scaled down in all dimensions. The Super Pullover often is found combined with a Torso-Arm attachment, but this will do you little good if you need the women's version.

It's not just height that makes the Super Pullover off limits for women. It's your narrow shoulder width and shorter lower and upper arm segments. To get a good picture of what the proper fit looks like, watch a 5'8" male use the machine. Note that when his elbows are in the elbow pads, several inches of upper arm also contact the pad. In other words, the long axis of his upper arm (elbow to shoulder) is only slightly off the long axis of the pad.

If you're about 5'2" or less, climb into the Super Pullover and note that, with your elbows on the pads, your upper arms are 30-degrees or so off the pad's long axis. What's worse, your elbows may not even reach the pads.

If you're not much taller than five feet, the best (and obvious) choice is the Women's Pullover. Failing that, try the Behind-Neck machine (hopefully paired with its Torso-Arm attachment). Failing that, expect near-miracles if you do conscientious work on a chinning bar. Yes, even 88-pound weaklings can shape and define through negative chins (see The Multiexercise Machine Chin-Ups, pages 54–57).

Since the actual Pullover movement is identical on both the Super and Women's machines, here are the instructions for both:

1. Before entering the machine, move one arm in the Pullover motion to visualize and estimate the center of shoulder rotation.
2. Sit in the machine and, with a spotter's help, position the seat so that your shoulder's axis of rotation matches the machine's axis (which you must also guess at).
3. Sit with your back firmly pressed against the seat back and buckle up.
4. Press the foot pedal down slowly to bring the bar around for you to grasp. If your height is 5'1" or below, you may need assistance. Bring the elbow pads down to about chest level.
5. Place your elbows on the pads. Your hands should be placed alongside the bars rising from the elbow pads. *Do not grasp and pull with this bar.* If you feel at all uncomfortable in this position (and you're in a men's machine), get out before you get hurt.
6. Remove your legs from the foot pedal and slowly let the weight stack pull you back into a stretched position. Do this only to the point that discomfort begins. Do not use the weight stack to increase your range of motion by 30-degrees!
7. Slowly, with the force applied *through your elbows,*

Pullover Machine, starting position.
1. Get a full but pain-free extension here.
2. Keep the back flat against the seat.

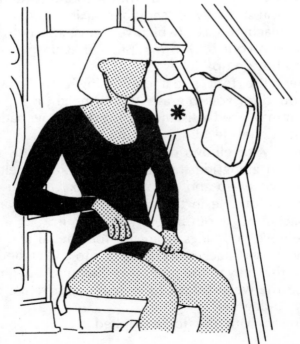

Shoulder and Cam Alignment—estimate the axis of shoulder rotation and match it with the cam axis (asterisk).

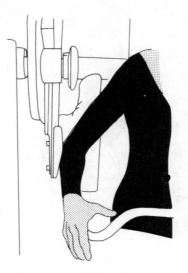

*The arms should be placed alongside
the bars. Do not pull with the hands;
push with the elbows.*

    rotate the bar down to your midsection or thighs (depending on your size).

8. Pause in the contracted position for a full second, then return slowly to the stretched position. Don't tense your head or neck or lean forward. Think slow, not throw. If you throw the weights around, you're throwing away the benefits.

9. Continue to momentary muscular failure or any unusual pain in the shoulder area. Injury incidence is extremely low when Nautilus equipment is used correctly, but this is one of the machines to be extra careful on. The shoulder joint is a very shallow ball-and-socket arrangement, and it is held together in a complex and injury-susceptible way. Be careful!

If you fit the Super (Men's) Pullover, and it has the Torso-Arm attachment, use it! This is another example of the Preexhaustion principle. Remember that you must shift *rapidly* from Pullover to Pulldown.

10. Quickly lower the Pullover seat as far as possible. This

Torso Arm exercise.
1. *Lower the seat to increase the range of motion.*
2. *Keep your back flat against the seat.*
3. *Pull the bar to the chest with the palms facing in.*

can and should be done without removing the safety belt. Lowering the seat allows the fullest possible range of motion on the Pulldown.

11. Have a spotter bring you the Pulldown bar. Grasp it with your palms facing you.
12. With your back pressed against the seat back to prevent arching, slowly pull the bar down as far as possible.
13. Pause for one full second in the contracted position, then slowly return to the fully stretched position. Repeat to momentary muscular failure.

THE MULTIEXERCISE MACHINE CHIN-UPS
Primary muscles worked: latissimus dorsi, teres major and minor, elbow flexors (biceps, brachialis)

This is a great alternative if you don't have a Women's Pullover to turn to. If you're not capable of doing four or more Chins from a fully stretched starting position, start with negative-only Chins. If you're mentally tough here, you'll develop a great back shape as well as the ability to do a surprising number of standard Chins. Negative Chins come as close to offering guaranteed results as possible. A former research assistant of mine and I watched this work on two private-school classes of six- to eight-year-old girls!

1. Bring the chinning bar over from the back position to rest in the forward position.
2. By raising the right and left adjustment levers, and placing one shoulder under the carriage, raise or lower the carriage so that when you're standing on the top step your chin is just over the chinning bar. This obviously requires some trial and error.
3. Grasp the chinning bar with palms facing you, placed a bit farther apart than shoulder width.
4. With your chin over the bar and your grip secure, lift your feet off the steps by flexing at the knee and start lowering yourself very slowly. Shoot for a slow count backward from 10. This works best if you count out loud, or have a partner do it. It gets tougher as you drop lower, so hang in there.
5. When you reach the fully stretched position, climb the steps and repeat from step 3. Keep these up until you have no control whatsoever over downward movement. Shoot for a minimum of five negatives.
6. For variety you may rotate the chinning bar into its back position and do negative Chins from the two parallel bars above and to your right and left. Palms should face each other. These are known as Parallel Grip Chins.
7. After about nine workouts, take a shot at standard Chin-Ups. If you can do four or five, begin your latissimus exercise from now on with these, then add at least five negative-only Chins.
8. If you're after masochistic pleasure or maximal muscular development, you may do weighted Chins by using the waist belt and the weight stack. Follow instructions as noted above for standard or negative only Chins.

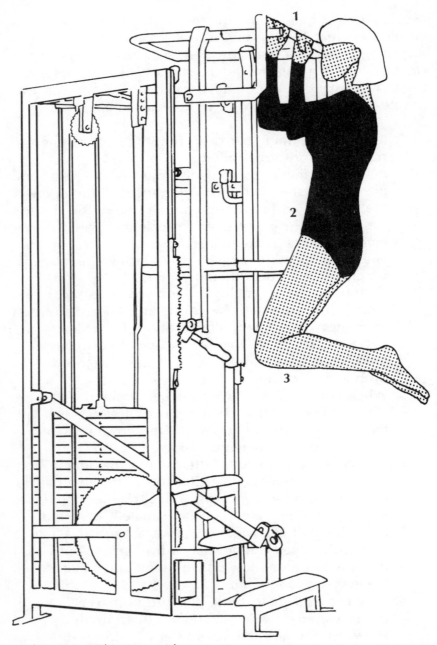

Multiexercise, Chin-Ups, mid-range.
1. Keep the palms facing in and place them just outside the shoulders.
2. Keep your abdominal and lower back muscles contracted and firm.
3. Keep the knees flexed to allow a full range of motion.

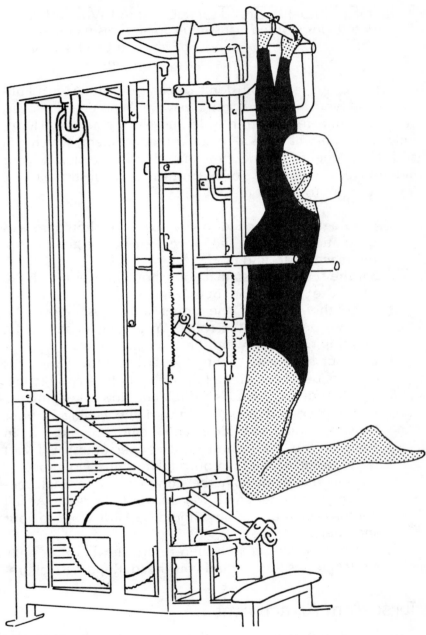

Chin-Ups, finishing position.

THE BEHIND-NECK/TORSO-ARM MACHINE

Primary muscles worked: latissimus dorsi, teres major and
minor; biceps and brachialis on
torso-arm movement

As noted above, if you don't or can't use the Men's Pull-over, and your facility doesn't have a Women's Pullover, you'll get fine results from a Behind-Neck machine. Hopefully, this unit will have a Torso-Arm attachment, which will add the benefits of the preexhaustion principle. If your Behind-Neck unit is *sans* Torso Arm, you may substitute Chins if you can get to them quickly.

1. Here again you'll need to visualize your shoulder's axis of rotation. Simulate the movement before getting into the machine to find it.
2. Set the seat height so that your shoulder axes match the cams' axes of rotation. Buckle in.
3. Place the backs of the upper arms, just above the elbows, on top of the rollers. Your fingers should be pointing roughly toward the ceiling.
4. Let your head lean slightly forward to allow your arms to cross behind it. Get a full stretch before contracting.
5. Slowly squeeze the pads around and down, keeping the hands back and pointing toward the ceiling. If your forearms and hands drop and begin pointing out in front of you, your chest muscles (pectoralis) will start taking some of the load off the latissimus. No good!
6. As you move through the contraction the angle between your upper and lower arms will decrease. At full contraction your thumbs should be fairly close to your shoulders.
7. Pause for a full second, then return slowly to the fully stretched position behind your head. Repeat to failure.

Torso-Arm Attachment

8. Lower the seat as far as possible while keeping the safety belt fastened.

Behind-Neck/Torso-Arm, Behind-Neck exercise, mid-range.
1. Keep the hands and forearms pointed toward the ceiling.
2. Keep the back flat against the seat.

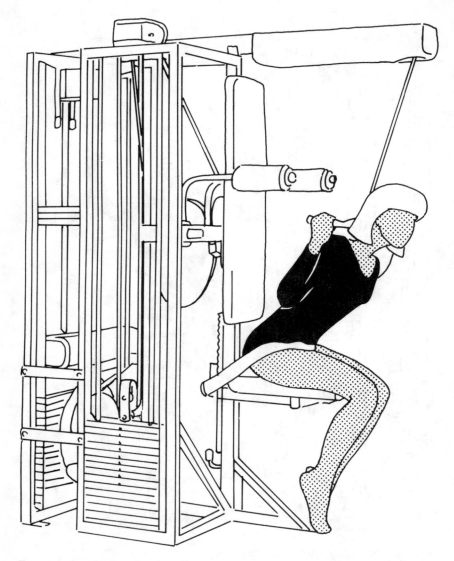

Torso-Arm exercise, finishing position. Lean forward and pull the bar (with palms facing in) to the shoulders.

9. Have a spotter pull the bar down to where you can grasp the handles with a parallel grip (palms facing each other).
10. Lean forward and pull the bar down behind you until it gently reaches your neck. Keep your elbows back.

11. Pause for a full second at full contraction, then slowly return the bar to the fully stretched position. Move slowly and with control in both directions. Avoid sudden or jerky movements like the plague! Repeat to failure.

THE ROWING TORSO MACHINE
Primary muscles worked: rear deltoids, trapezius

These are two neglected muscle groups that nevertheless play an important role in upper body posture. Don't avoid this machine!

1. Sit with your back toward the weight stack. Only use seat pads to raise yourself if your elbows don't make full contact with the rollers.
2. I prefer to sit against the forward pad rather than the back, since it gives me an object against which to push. I recommend this over sitting back.
3. Thread your arms through the rollers and place them on the rollers just above your elbows. Let your hands/forearms cross one another so that you get a full stretch across the back.
4. Slowly move your elbows outward and back while keeping your arms perfectly parallel to the floor. The angle between upper and lower arms will decrease as you contract.
5. Pause for a full second at full contraction, then slowly return to the fully stretched position. Repeat to momentary muscular failure.

THE DOUBLE CHEST MACHINE and the Women's Chest Machine
Primary muscles worked: pectoralis major/minor, front deltoids; triceps on Incline Press exercise

Here's another machine that small women are advised to use carefully. Nautilus has finally introduced a Women's Chest machine to solve this problem.

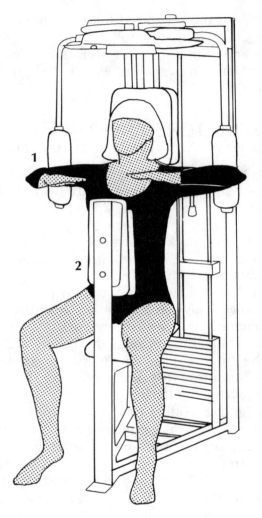

Rowing Torso.
1. Keep the arms parallel to the floor.
2. Sit against the forward pad.

The Double Chest uses the preexhaustion principle to blow out the pectoralis group. For some obscure reason Nautilus calls the secondary movement the Decline Press. Sorry, but it's an Incline Press. Decline benches place the head *lower* than the feet, inclines higher. This is international convention, so I'm going to call it the Incline Press.

The Arm Cross Exercise

1. You have two adjustments to worry about here. The first is seat height. The seat should be positioned so that you can grasp the movement arms and maintain a 90-degree angle between the upper and lower arms. This is the easy one, though. The hard one is lining up with the overhead cams.

2. The goal here is to keep your shoulders directly below the overhead cams. Sitting with your back flat against the seat, bring your arms forward, without the movement arms, to their final position in front of you. Have a spotter check where your shoulders lie relative to the axis of the overhead cams. Your shoulder axes should lie directly below the cam axes. Many women will need a long back pad behind them to shimmy them forward.

3. These two things accomplished, strap in.

4. Keep your back flat and your feet up on the ledge just below the seat bottom. Place your hands and forearms in position on the movement arms. Hook your thumbs under the handles but keep the other fingers back. There is no need to grip the handles with all five fingers; in fact, you'll get better results by avoiding doing so.

5. If you've followed directions to this point, and a good part of your forearm isn't on the movement arm pads, you're too small. Get off. Using a Women's machine or doing Push-Ups are your alternatives.

6. After buckling in, push with your forearms and slowly try to touch your elbows in front of you. *Always keep your elbows directly under, or even inside, the hands.*

7. Pause a full second at this finishing position, then return slowly to the fully stretched position. If you can bottom out the weight stack, touch and go. No resting between reps. Repeat to momentary muscular failure.

8. This exercise may be done unilaterally (one arm at a time) if the free hand grasps the U-shaped handle above each shoulder. This might work well for women who are too small to use the machine bilaterally (two at a time).

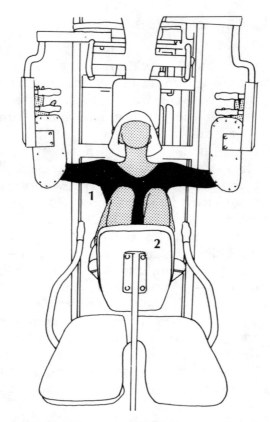

Double Chest unit, Arm Cross exercise, mid-range.
1. Maintain a 90-degree angle between the torso and upper arms.
2. Keep the feet up to lessen strain on the back.

The Incline Press Exercise

9. Immediately place both feet on the foot pedal and press out to bring the handles into position from behind you.
10. Your hands should be at or just below breast level. Use a palms-facing or hands-on-top grip to achieve this. Release the foot pedal and extend smoothly but do not lock out elbows.
11. Lower the weights slowly with the elbows kept wide.

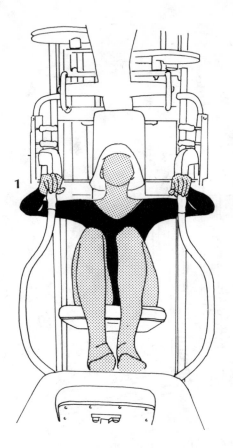

Double Chest, Incline Press exercise, mid-range.
1. Place the hands on the levers at mid-chest height.

Get as complete a stretch as possible, then slowly repeat. Go to momentary failure as always.

The Women's Chest Machine

1. This is a reduced-size version of the men's machine but
   comes without the Incline Press. You should only have
   to worry about seat height here, but have a spotter
   check your shoulders against the overhead cams any-
   way. Perform as described above for the men's unit.

Women's Chest, near finishing position.
1. *Keep the hands open.*
2. *Maintain a 90-degree bend in the elbow.*
3. *Keep the head back and relaxed.*

THE 10-DEGREE CHEST MACHINE
Primary muscles worked: pectoralis major and minor, front
deltoids

1. Lie on your back with your head toward the weight
   stack. Place your feet on the small platform and begin
   to position yourself by placing your upper arms under
   the roller pads. Keep the rollers in, or slightly above,
   the crook of the elbow and the forearms pointing
   toward the ceiling.
2. With your arms now positioned, move your body up or
   back on the seat to create a 90-degree angle between
   the upper arms and the torso.

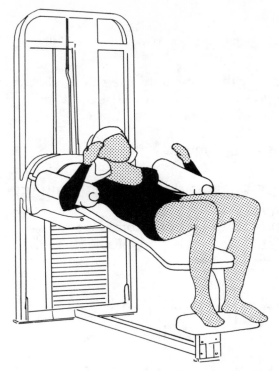

10-Degree Chest, mid-range. Keep the arms flexed at the elbow.

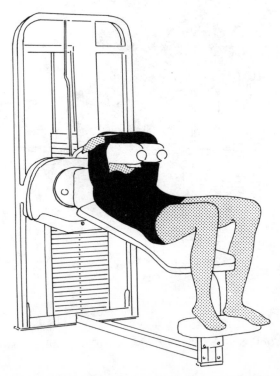

10-Degree Chest, finishing position. Get the full range of motion.

3. Contract the arms until the rollers almost touch above the chest. Pause for a full second, then return to the stretched position. Touch and go if you can bottom the weights out.
4. Repeat to momentary muscular failure.

THE 40-DEGREE CHEST/SHOULDER MACHINE

Primary muscles worked: pectoralis major and minor, front and middle deltoids

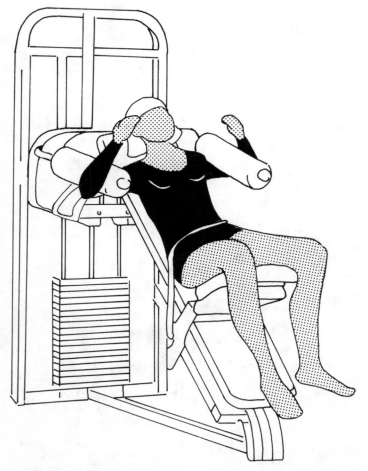

40-Degree Chest/Shoulder, mid-range. Keep the arms flexed at the elbow.

1. Have a spotter help you set the seat height. The tops of your shoulders should line up with the axes of the cams. Buckle up.
2. Place the arms exactly as you did on the 10-Degree Chest machine above.
3. Contract and slowly bring the pads toward each other. Pause in this position, then return slowly to a full stretch. Touch and go if you can bottom out. Work to momentary muscular failure.

40-Degree Chest/Shoulder, finishing position. Full contraction overhead!

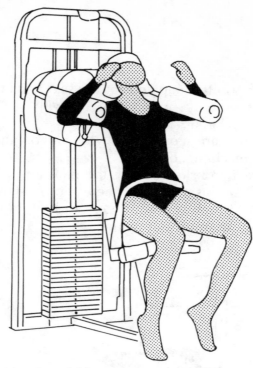

70-Degree Shoulder unit, mid-range. Keep the arms flexed at the elbow.

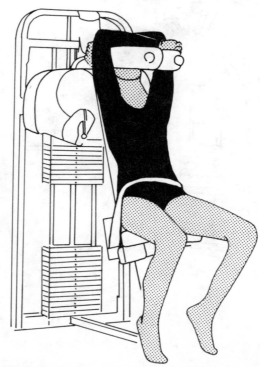

70-Degree Shoulder, finishing position. Get the full range of motion of the exercise.

THE 70-DEGREE SHOULDER MACHINE
Primary muscles worked: front, middle, and rear deltoids;
trapezius

1. Arm position, hand position, and seat height are set as on the 10-Degree and 40-Degree units. Buckle up.
2. Lean your head back and rest it on the pad behind your shoulders. You should be gazing at the ceiling.
3. Contract as on the 10-Degree and 40-Degree machines, bringing the elbows nearly together over your face.
4. Pause, hold, and then return to a full stretch. Touch and go if you can bottom out. Work, as always, to failure.

THE DOUBLE SHOULDER MACHINE
Primary muscles worked: front, middle, and rear deltoids;
triceps on the Overhead Press
exercise

The Lateral Raise Exercise

1. Get yourself a spotter—seat height adjustment here requires outside help. The seat should be positioned such that the axes of shoulder rotation (simulate the movement outside the machine to find them) match the axes of cam rotation.
2. Thread your hands and forearms between the pads and handles. Your hands should not close around the handles. You will be applying pressure with the back of the hands, wrists, and lower forearms. Buckle in.
3. Keeping your back firmly pressed into the seat, lift by leading with your elbows. Raise your arms *no farther* than parallel to the floor. Keep the shoulders relaxed and down.
4. Pause and hold this position. Lower slowly, remembering to touch and go. For some unknown reason, this exercise seems to cause more intense pain than any exercise done on any other Nautilus machine. You'll want to rest between reps. Don't give in!
5. Continue, always at slow speed, to momentary failure.

Double Shoulder, Lateral Raise exercise, starting position.
1. Keep the grips open.
2. Keep the shoulders down. Rotate the elbows upward without shrugging the shoulders.
3. Keep the head back and relaxed.

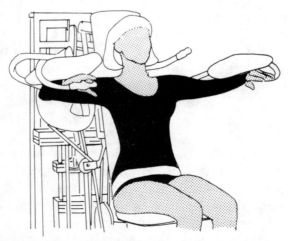

Double Shoulder, Lateral Raise, finishing position.

The Overhead Press Exercise

Many smaller women have difficulty with even one rep on the Overhead Press unit. Give it a try, for it will really speed results. You can also have a spotter lift the weights for you to allow negatives.

6. Ideally one should rapidly lift the seat to its highest position after finishing the Lateral Raise. The higher you are for the Press, the lower the Overhead Press handles are relative to your shoulders. This will give you a fuller range of motion. If you can manage at least five reps with the seat up, go for it. If you can't, leave the seat at its Lateral Raise setting and do as many as you can through this reduced, and therefore easier, range of motion.

Double Shoulder, Overhead Press exercise, mid-range.
1. Keep the hands loose or open.
2. Keep the head back and relaxed.

7. Grasp the handles with an open, parallel grip.
8. Press the handles overhead while keeping the back pressed into the seat. Don't arch your back!
9. Stop just before locking out the elbows. You *won't* want to after lowering the weights, but touch and go. No rest for the weary between reps! Go to momentary muscular failure.

THE ROTARY TORSO MACHINE
Primary muscles worked: internal and external obliques, transverse abdominus, spinal erectors

This is a nifty way to train the obliques, those muscles that form a crosshatched girdle around your midsection. It's a machine that most people use incorrectly, so take special care.

1. Some of these machines come with a rotating seat, others with a seat that extends right *and* left of the weight stack. If yours falls into the former category, adjust the seat so that it's 90-degrees to the right or left of the weight stack.
2. Before doing anything else, visualize an axis of rotation running down through your body from head to heel. Picture your torso rotating around this axis while you're seated. That is the essence of this exercise.
3. Sit in the machine and rotate your torso around that imaginary axis to face the movement arm/arm pad assembly. *You should not be leaning over; you should be rotating around.*
4. Place your forearms on the pads and let your hands cross and grasp the opposite bars (right hand on left bar and vice versa).
5. *Left* will mean the left side of the weight stack as you're facing it. If you're sitting and facing the left side, you are going to rotate your torso from your left to your right. Use pressure of the left hand, but turn with your

Rotary Torso.
1. The right hand is on the left bar and vice versa.
2. Keep your gaze between the two bars.

torso. If you keep your visual gaze directly between the two vertical bars, and your hands always in front of the middle of your chest, this will be easy.

6. Only rotate as far as your torso allows. This is a torso, *not* an arm, exercise. When your torso can no longer rotate and move the weights, don't attempt to rotate the movement arm farther with your arms.

7. As always, pause and hold in the contracted position, then return slowly to full stretch or to weight stack bottom-out (remember, touch and go). Work to momentary failure on one side, then switch to the other side for another complete set to failure.

THE ABDOMINAL MACHINE
Primary muscles worked: abdominals; psoas and rectus femoris (hip flexors)

This machine has really captured people's imaginations, but it's not exactly the brightest star in the Nautilus heavens. As it is currently designed, a great deal of the load that *should* be borne by the abdominals is instead shared or borne by the hip flexors and the latissimus dorsi and upper arms.

When you anchor your feet in a Sit-Up maneuver, you automatically enable the hip flexors (psoas and rectus femoris) to assist the contraction. The rage of the Sit-Up world is the unanchored-foot Sit-Up, and rightly so, for it tremendously increases the abdominal loading while reducing psoas and rectus involvement. Try this test for yourself right now:

Get down on the floor (on your back), bend your knees up toward the ceiling, and keep your feet flat on the floor at least 12 inches from your buttocks. Perform a few Sit-Ups and feel the intensity of abdominal work. Now find a couch or spotter to anchor your feet. Try a few more Sit-Ups, and you'll be shocked to find that they become about 50 percent easier. Since the lower body is anchored on the Nautilus Abdominal machine, your abs will have to share the work with your psoas and rectus.

Part two of the problem is that the current design requires that you grasp two handles above you and to the right and

Abdominal machine.
1. *Keep the knees spread as wide as possible.*
2. *Pass the arms through the handles.*
3. *Concentrate on contracting here.* Do not *pull with the arms and legs.*

left. Though you're told not to pull with the arms to contract, it's nearly impossible not to do so. The abdominals now end up sharing the load with the psoas, the rectus, the latissimus, and several smaller torso muscles.

Despite all these complaints, the unit is probably the safest and best way to progressively increase loading on the muscles that flex the body at the hip.

1. You'll need a spotter to help you with seat height. First find the axis of cam rotation. You'll need to peek around behind and inside the machine for this. Now locate the lower part of your sternum.
2. Set the seat so that the bottom tip of your sternum is at the same height as the cam axis.

3. Place your ankles behind the roller pads. Keeping your knees spread as far apart as possible will help reduce hip flexor involvement.
4. Instead of grasping the handles, continue moving your hands and forearms up through the space between handles and bars. If you now anchor your body with the sideward pressure of the arms, you'll be less able to pull with the torso musculature.
5. Concentrate on creating movement through abdominal muscle contraction only. Don't pull with your arms or legs. Think about crunching your abdominals down. This may take some time to learn, so be patient.
6. The range of motion of the rectus abdominus (what most people call the abdominals) is not as great as you think. It does *not* bring you from 180-degrees to 90-degrees. It can only contract for less than half that range, so you have to complete only about half the possible range of the Abdominal machine. As always, you'll see people trying to contract to the end of the machine's range. Just don't watch.
7. Pause at this midway point, hold for a full second, then return to the starting position. Remember, touch and go. Work to momentary failure. Always try to eliminate arm and leg action.

THE MULTIEXERCISE MACHINE SIDE BENDS
Primary muscles worked: internal and external obliques, spinal erectors

1. Find the short bar accessory for the Multiexercise machine. Attach it as closely as possible to the movement arm.
2. Stand at a right angle to the steps of the machine, with your closest leg an inch or two away from the bottom step.
3. Grasp the handle with your palm facing your leg. Stand up and position yourself so that you are leaning in a perfect left-to-right plane. Place the opposite hand on

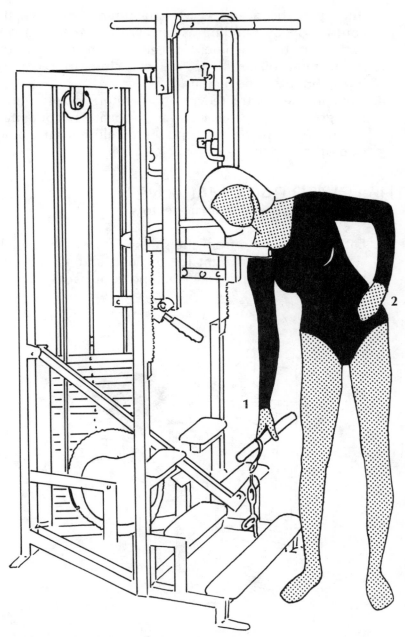

Multiexercise, Side Bends, starting position.
1. *Grasp the bar with the palm in.*
2. *Move only in a side-to-side plane. Don't lean forward or back.*

the hip or head and slowly straighten. Complete the contraction by bending as far as possible to the side away from the machine. Concentrate on staying in the left-to-right plane. Keep the bar close to the body throughout the movement.

4. Hold in the contracted position, return slowly (touch and go if you bottom out), and repeat to momentary failure. Turn and do a second set to failure for the other side of the body.

THE LOWER BACK MACHINE
Primary muscles worked: spinal erectors

1. Enter the machine from the side away from the weight stack. Thread your right leg through and straddle the seat. Keep the upper roller behind your back.

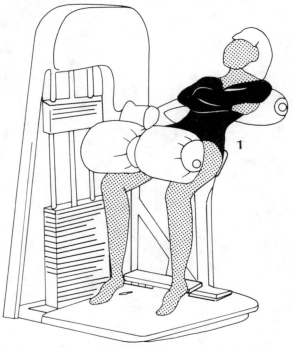

Lower Back, finishing position.
1. Contract to the point where your torso and thighs form a straight line.

2. Find a comfortable and stable position for your legs. For the shorter people out there, you may want to wedge your legs between the rollers and the elevated foot platform. Taller folks will probably use the rollers and the main platform. Rotate the off-center rollers to keep you snugly in place.

3. After strapping in, cross your arms on your chest. Slowly and smoothly move your torso back until your torso and upper thighs form a straight line. Pause and hold for a full second.

4. Return slowly to the starting position, touch and go, and repeat to momentary muscular failure. Back off at any sign of unusual pain.

CHAPTER 6

THE ARMS

There are only three body areas to concentrate on here: biceps (the front of the upper arm), triceps (back of the upper arm), and forearms. Remember here again that while Nautilus *can* tone, strengthen, and/or add muscle, it *can't* make the fat magically disappear. If you find yourself with flabby arms, combine your strength training with calorie control.

THE MULTIBICEPS MACHINE
Primary muscles worked: elbow flexors (biceps, brachialis),
forearm flexors

The sadists/designers down at Nautilus have worked at least eight different exercise possibilities into the Multibiceps and Multitriceps machines. I recommend that you spend some time with the simpler options before experimenting with the more difficult ones. (Consider the first three, below, your starting point.) Let's review the instructions common to all eight first, then consider special points exercise by exercise.

1. Sit on the seat with your legs straddling the bar. Place both elbows on the pad and align their axes with the cam axes.
2. When you're correctly seated, your elbows should be slightly higher than your shoulders. Get off the machine and raise or lower the seat as necessary. Record this setting.
3. Stand straddling the seat, reach forward, and grasp both

handles. Now sit and maintain a perfectly straight line, angled upward, between shoulder and hands. This eliminates the problem of finding and handling levers that are several inches below your hands when you're positioned correctly.

Two-Arm Normal

1. Keeping the shoulders relaxed and down, curl both arms to the shoulders simultaneously. Keep your elbows aligned with the cam axes. If your shoulders tend to rise, reduce the weight.
2. Pause in the fully contracted position. Return slowly to the straight-line starting position (shoulder to hand). Keep the shoulders down and work to momentary muscular failure.

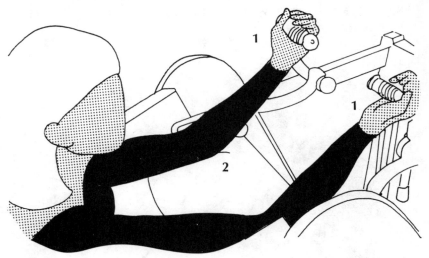

Multibiceps, Bilateral variation.
1. Both arms extend and curl up simultaneously.
2. Keep the elbow axes at the cam axes.

Two-Arm Alternate

1. Do one complete Curl with the left arm while the right arm remains extended.

2. Pause at full contraction, then return to meet the right arm.
3. Perform 12 contractions (go to failure) with each arm. Keep the shoulders down.

Two-Arm Duo Poly

1. With shoulders down and elbows in proper position, curl both arms to the shoulders.
2. Holding the right hand at the shoulder, slowly lower the left arm to the 180-degree starting position, then curl it back to the shoulder.
3. Now holding the left hand at the shoulder, do one rep with the right arm. This is probably the most popular use of the Multibiceps machine, though there are no comparative research data to support the practice.
4. Perform 12 reps with each arm, or go to failure if you haven't reached it by 12.

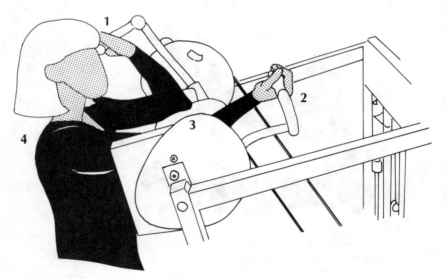

Multibiceps, Duo-Poly variation.
1. The left arm holds isometrically, while. . .
2. . . . the right arm extends, then curls up with an open grip.
3. Keep the elbow axes at the cam axes.
4. Keep the shoulders from shrugging.

One-Arm Normal

1. Grasping just one of the levers, with the other arm resting on the elbow pad, do a complete set of Curls to momentary failure. Keep the elbow in place and the shoulder down. Switch to the other arm and repeat to failure.

One-Arm Negative Only

1. As in One Arm Normal above, you're going to work one arm at a time. Here, however, the resting arm will be used *with* the contracting arm to bring the weight to the shoulder. This will be useful for two kinds of people: those who are rehabilitating a weakened arm and cannot curl even one plate and those who are interested in gaining maximal strength through heavy negatives.
2. You will have to stand to bring the weight to the shoulder with both hands. Once there, sit and recheck the elbow and shoulders.
3. To a slow count backward from 10, return the weight to the 180-degree starting position. In a rehabilitation setting a spotter should be present to take the weight at any moment. Do not rest between reps. Stand and bring the weight to the shoulders for the next rep.
4. Work to the point at which you can no longer control the downward descent of the weight stack, then switch arms.
5. Expect to use 20–40 percent more weight with negatives than you do with standard curls.

Infimetric and Akinetic

The Multibiceps and Multitriceps machines, like some Duo-Squat units, have a restraining bar that swings into place above the weight stack. This will allow infimetric (arm against arm suspending only one plate) and akinetic (arm against arm suspending more than one plate) work.

Though there are some logical and intuitive reasons to anticipate superior results with these kinds of contractions, there are as yet no supportive data.

Infimetric:
1. Remove the pin from the weight stack and swing the restraining bar into place above the stack. Position yourself as for a Two-Arm Curl.
2. Curling both arms to midrange will bring one weight plate up to the restraining bar.
3. You must keep the plate against the restraining bar until momentary muscular failure. The exercise involves curling (flexing) one arm slowly while the other arm resists in the opposite direction. Pulling or curling with your right arm, for example, extends or pulls out on the left arm. Since the extending (left) arm is always physiologically able to produce 30–40 percent *more* force than the curling arm the left arm in this example *could* completely stop the right arm from curling. *Don't* try this. The trick is to use the left arm to give the right a "hard time." Provide enough resistance to keep the movement slow and the plate against the restraining bar. Follow the same principle when the left arm is curling and the right is extending.
4. Alternate flexing and extending through the full range until you can no longer keep the plate against the restraining bar.

   Hint: Try gradually slowing your speed of movement through the set. This enables you to create more force and will allow a few extra reps before failure.

Akinetic:
1. The only difference between infimetric and akinetic is that here you're going to throw some weight "between the arms" to make it more difficult. Try this with the pin set at only two or three plates before you go any further.
2. Watching shoulders and elbow position as above, curl one arm and resist with the other. Keep the weight

stack in constant contact with the restraining bar. Failure means the inability to accomplish this.

Isometric:
1. Set up as for infimetric work. Isometrics, or contractions without movement, are possible because the extending arm is 30–40 percent stronger than the flexing arm.
2. Bring the single plate up to the restraining bar by curling the arms simultaneously to midrange. Now position the right arm about halfway between full extension (180-degrees) and 90-degrees. Contract it as forcefully as possible for about six to eight seconds but prevent it from moving with the left arm.
3. Rest for about 15 seconds, then move the right arm to about a 90-degree angle. Repeat as in step 2.
4. Rest for 15 seconds, then move the right arm about half of the remaining distance to the shoulder (45-degrees between upper and lower arms). This is the last rep done with the right arm.
5. Move the left arm to its first position (halfway between 180-degrees and 90-degrees) and follow steps 2–4 again.
6. At the next workout, begin with the left arm and follow with the right.

THE MULTITRICEPS MACHINE
Primary muscles worked: triceps brachii

Except for the fact that you're going to extend your arms using your triceps, the exercise variations on this machine are identical to those of the Multibiceps. Instructions for all eight variations follow.

1. As for the Multibiceps, a straight line should be formed by the upper and lower arms, with the shoulders slightly lower than the elbows. Adjust the seat height with a spotter's help, if necessary.
2. Remember to keep the elbows aligned with the cam axes of rotation.
3. Your palms should be facing inward, or across your

body. *Do not* close your fingers around the end of the hand pad. Keep them extended as in a "karate chop" position.

The Variations

See Multibiceps for more detail.

Two-Arm Normal: Both arms will flex back to the shoulders, then extend simultaneously to 180 degrees.

Two-Arm Alternate: Keeping one arm flexed (relaxed at the shoulder, do a complete rep with the other arm, then reverse.

Two-Arm Duo Poly: Extend both arms. Keeping one isometrically contracted at extension, do a full rep with the other. Reverse.

One-Arm Normal: Work one arm at a time to failure. Keep the other arm resting on the elbow pad.

One-Arm Negative Only: Use the resting arm to help extend the working arm to 180-degrees. Lower to a slow count of

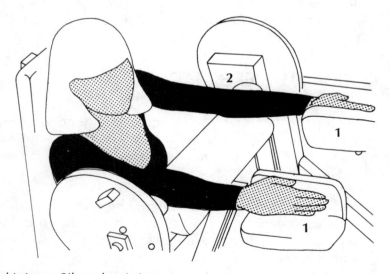

Multitriceps, Bilateral variation.
1. Both arms flex, then extend simultaneously.
2. Keep the elbow axes aligned with the cam axes.

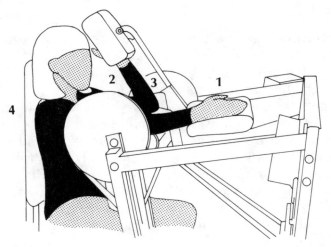

Multitriceps, Duo-Poly variation.
1. The right arm holds isometrically, while . . .
2. . . . the left arm flexes, then extends.
3. Keep the elbow axes in place.
4. Keep the shoulders from shrugging.

10. Repeat until the weight stack's descent cannot be controlled.

Infimetric and Akinetic: Swing the restraining bar into place. Extend both arms to midrange until the single plate or multiple plates contact the bar. Extend one arm and resist with the other.

Isometric: Use the restraining bar and the top weight plate only. Work each arm at 45, 90, and 135 degrees of extension.

THE PLATELOADING BICEPS-TRICEPS MACHINE

Primary muscles worked: elbow flexors (biceps, brachialis) and elbow extensors (triceps brachii)

This combination unit is the very popular forerunner of the Multibiceps and Multitriceps machines. Since the seats are not adjustable (you'll need pads), use the Multi machines if you have a choice.

Biceps Curl

1. Enter this machine *carefully*. It is easy to hurt yourself.
2. Place your elbows on the pad and line up their axes with the cam axis.
3. Grasp the bar with the palms up and the hands close together. Use the top bar (as you face the machine). Stand up if you must to get hold of the bar.
4. Keeping the shoulders down and relaxed, and the elbows in position, curl the bar smoothly to full flexion.
5. Pause for a full second, then return to the starting position. You may need to lean back slightly to get a full extension, but don't move your elbows!
6. Do not rest between reps. Continue to momentary failure.

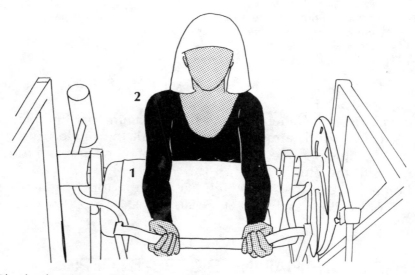

Plateloading Biceps/Triceps, Biceps Curl exercise.
1. Keep the elbow axes in place.
2. Keep the shoulders down.

Triceps Extension

1. This machine requires that the elbows and shoulders be at the same level. Use pads beneath you, if necessary, to elevate the shoulders. Get in carefully!

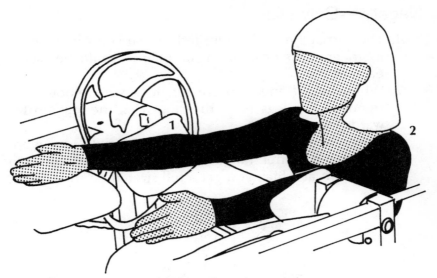

Plateloading Biceps/Triceps, Triceps Extension exercise.
1. Keep the elbow axis at the cam axis.
2. Keep the shoulders from shrugging.

2. Keeping your elbows aligned with the cam axis, place your hands, with palms facing each other, on the pads.
3. Extend arms smoothly to a 180-degree angle. Pause for a full second, then return slowly. Repeat to failure.

THE MULTIEXERCISE MACHINE TRICEPS DIPS

Primary muscles worked: triceps

Those two old standbys, Dips and Chin-Ups, are still on top of every expert's exercise list. The Multiexercise machine allows several effective variations of dips.

Chances are that most women will be unable to do a full set of standard Dips. (Chances are that most *males* can't, either, come to think of it.) Therefore, we'll start with negative-only Dips. Do they work? A young female swimmer I worked with recently went from two to 14 legal Dips in the space of 12 workouts, doing only negatives. Of course, she was working on other machines, but she *was* already in fine muscular shape. Trust me—they work!

Negative-Only Dips

1. The carriage must be adjusted so that you can climb to a straight-arm position. Your palms should be facing each other.
2. When height and grip are set, lock your elbows and remove your legs from the step. Flex the legs up towards your buttocks.
3. Lower as slowly and as deeply as possible, but work only in a pain-free range of motion. It is nice to drop to the point at which you get a full stretch on the triceps,

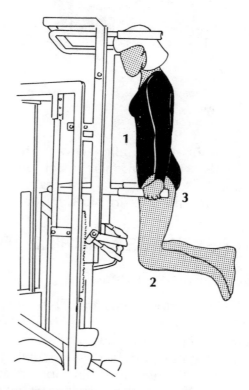

Multiexercise, Triceps Dips, starting position.
1. Keep the abdominals and lower back firm.
2. Keep the knees flexed.
3. Palms face inward.

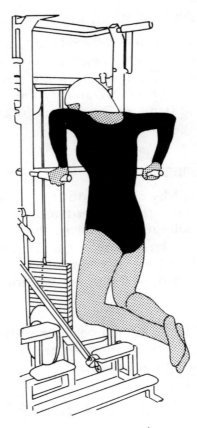

Triceps Dips, finishing position. Lower to a 90-degree angle between the upper and lower arms.

but many shoulders can't bear this. Try to dip to at least a 90-degree angle between the upper and lower arms. Climb back up the stairs and repeat.

4. Negatives are all mental. Count out loud or have a partner count out loud. Going backward from 10 seems to work best. Work until you can no longer control downward motion or to the onset of any unusual pain. If you have a history of shoulder problems, avoid this exercise completely.

Negative, Weighted Dips

The advanced trainee will not want to miss this one. This exercise is identical to the negative Dips described above, but the waist belt and weight stack are used to augment the downward pull of gravity. Don't try these until you can perform at least 10 standard Dips. Don't forget to take care with the weight belt; it must be snug.

Standard Dips

As above, start by climbing to the elbows-locked position. Simply lower and extend upward until momentary failure. It is better to do full-range negatives than halfhearted, partial-range standards. Have a spotter check how deep you're going on your standard Dips. If you can't do five legal Dips (a 90-degree angle between the upper and lower arms), switch to negatives.

Note for all Dips: Remember to pay attention to abnormal shoulder pain. These injuries can be tough to rehabilitate, so stop at the first sign of trouble.

THE MULTIEXERCISE MACHINE WRIST CURLS
Primary muscles worked: wrist flexors and extensors

The forearms are a neglected but important part of both daily living and athletic performance. The flexors and extensors are easy to train using the Multiexercise machine.

Wrist Flexors

1. Find the small bar and attach it to the movement arm. Find a chair or a low bench as well.
2. Bring the chair or bench close enough so that you sit facing the machine and your toes are under the lowest step.

Multiexercise, Wrist Curl exercise, starting position.
1. Only the wrists extend out past the knees. Palms face upward.

3. Reach down between your legs and grasp the bar with your palms facing up. Lift the bar above the knees, bring your knees together, and lay your forearms on your thighs. Only your hands should extend out over the leg.
4. With only your hands moving, lower the bar for a full stretch of the forearms. Curl slowly up to maximal flexion and hold. Lower slowly and repeat to momentary muscular failure.

Wrist Extensors

These are called *Reverse Wrist Curls,* since your palms will now face down. The exercise is identical to the Wrist Flexors but for this difference. Expect to use a lower weight for this exercise, since the extensors are weaker than the flexors.

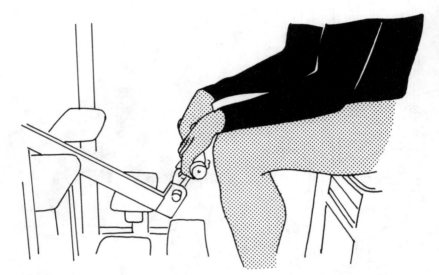

Multiexercise, Reverse Wrist Curls, starting position. Note the reversed grip!

CHAPTER 7

THE NECK

Talk about neglected areas! Weakness in the neck muscula-ture may surface in any number of ways. A model I worked with recently on a photo shoot found herself unable to hold her head up while doing a Push-Up. In talking, I discovered that she often suffered from headaches and neckaches after a day at her office desk. Muscular integrity of the neck is probably *most* important, though, in times of accident or trauma.

When asked why nonathletic women needed to train their necks, Ken Hutchins of Nautilus Florida would always re-spond: "Are they ever in cars?" In that rare instance when we find ourselves in an accident at home or in a car, muscular integrity of the neck can prevent severe cervical spine dam-age or even death.

An athletic friend of mine just recently totaled his one-day-old sports car after being forced into a tree at 40 miles per hour. He survived with a few broken ribs and some lung and heart bruises, but the attending doctors were unanimous in stating that his excellent muscular fitness saved his life. I've seen 10 instances of this if I've seen one.

Even though most of you won't learn your lesson from this sermon, you should learn to use the three Nautilus neck machines.

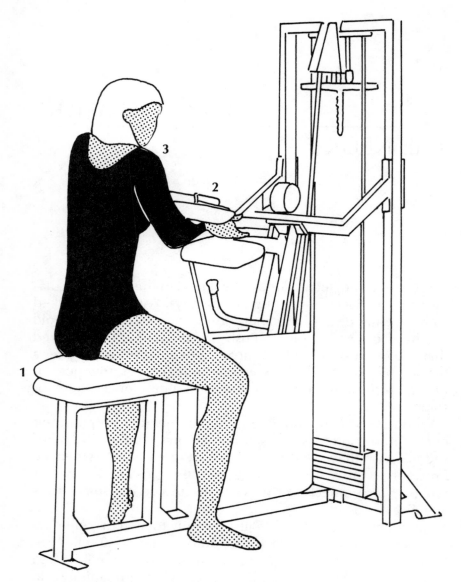

Neck and Shoulder.
1. *Use enough pads to lift the weight load you're using off the stack in the starting position.*
2. *Palms face up.*
3. *Now you can hunch your shoulders!*

THE NECK AND SHOULDER MACHINE

Primary muscles worked: trapezius and neck extensors

1. Place your forearms between the pads while seated. Palms face up and extend out over the pads. Pressure will be exerted by the top surface of the forearm, near the elbow.
2. Sit up with your back straight, holding your abdominals in for support. If, in this position, the weight load you have chosen is not completely elevated off the rest of the stack, get off the machine and find some small pads to sit on. You may need two or three to elevate you sufficiently.
3. This exercise is called a *Shrug,* for you'll be training the trapezius and neck by shrugging your shoulders as high as possible. Do not lift with your biceps. Always keep your elbows by your sides. Practice this movement while off the machine, if necessary.
4. Pause at full contraction, lower slowly to the fully stretched position, then repeat to failure.
5. Remember, don't bottom the weight stack out. If you can do this, you're sitting too low.

THE FOUR-WAY NECK MACHINE

Primary muscles worked: anterior flexors, posterior extensors, lateral flexors (right and left)

This is a nifty piece of equipment that will allow you to train neck contraction in four directions. Many of you will find that even the minimum weight load is too much for you to handle. There is nothing wrong with using your own hand or a spotter to help you through the contractions.

Be especially careful on these machines to always use proper form. Have a spotter check you out periodically, if not at every workout.

Anterior Flexion (chin toward chest)

1. Sit on the seat so that you are looking at the two face pads. Adjust seat height so that your nose is in the exact center of the opening when your face is pressed into the pads.
2. Stabilize yourself with the hand grips to your right and left. Spot yourself with one hand, or use a spotter, until you are sure that your anterior flexors can handle the load.
3. Keeping your torso absolutely steady, bring your head slowly and smoothly toward your chest.
4. Pause in this position for a full second, then let the head stretch back as far as possible while keeping the torso motionless. Repeat to failure or any abnormal pain.

Posterior Extension (head leaning backward)

1. Turn 180-degrees so that the back of your head now sits squarely against the face pads.
2. Stabilize yourself with the left and right handles. Again, use one hand or a spotter until you are confident that the posterior extensors can do the job alone.
3. Keeping the torso perfectly steady, lean the head back as far as possible. Hold in the contracted position, then let the head stretch forward to the chest. Repeat to momentary failure or any unusual pain.

Lateral Flexion (to right and left shoulders)

1. Turn 90-degrees to either side so that one ear fits squarely between the face pads.
2. Stabilize with the right and left handles. Use a spotter or one hand for safety.
3. Again keeping your torso rock-steady and upright, tilt the head to one side to the position of full contraction. Hold for a full second, then return slowly to get a good stretch of the contracting side.

Four-Way Neck.
1. Keep the torso perfectly upright. Bend only at the neck.
2. Use the right and left handles for stability or use one hand to hold the bar near your head for safety.

THE ROTARY NECK MACHINE
Primary muscles worked: neck rotators

In this unique machine you will use your arms to provide resistance for negative contractions of your neck rotators.

1. First, familiarize yourself with the overhead lever that adjusts the head pads and the right and left levers that rotate the head pads.
2. Sit facing away from the machine with the two long levers to your sides.
3. Place your head between the pads and tighten them by pulling the overhead lever from left to right. (Some think this machine was actually a medieval torture device.) Make it a snug fit.
4. The concept here is that when you push the right-hand lever (and/or pull the left lever) the head will be forced to rotate to the left, and vice versa. Your goal is to resist your arms with the muscles that rotate the neck. In other words, pushing the right-hand lever will enable negative-only training of the neck muscles that prevent rotation to the left (the right-side rotators).
5. After a maximal-range contraction to the left, reverse direction with your arms. Push with your left arm and pull with your right to force head rotation to the right and a negative load on the *left*-side rotators.
6. Your goal is six repetitions to each side for a total of twelve. Since there's no weight load to increase, you're on the honor system here—give 100 percent *every* time you perform this exercise, on *every* rep.
7. Release the head pads by moving the overhead lever from left to right. Don't ask me how you're supposed to remember that after a hard set; I personally keep a spotter handy to get me out.

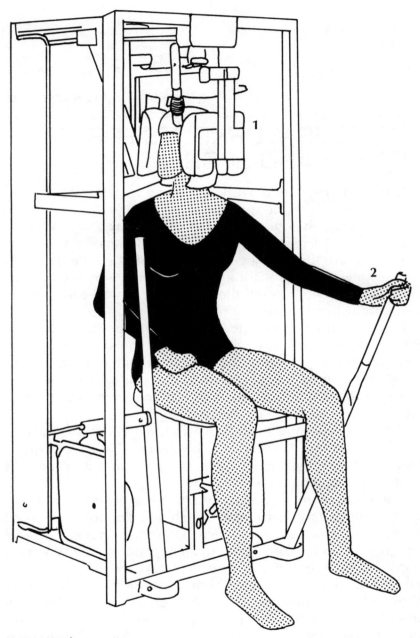

Rotary Neck.
1. *Get a snug fit around the head.*
2. *Pushing the left lever rotates the head to the right. You are thereby training the muscles on the left side of the neck.*

CHAPTER 8

NAUTILUS WORKOUTS FOR FITNESS AND SPORT

Here's the payoff—10 workouts plus suggestions on Nautilus training for specific sports.

How should they be used? If you're a newcomer to Nautilus, you'll want to spend one or two months on your first workout plan. If you're a good student, all the little details in the last few chapters will be ingrained in you by the conclusion of this period. You'll then be ready to start experimenting with higher-intensity training.

If you're already in shape, and you've been strength training on other types of equipment, give yourself a month or less before venturing out on the road to high intensity. Don't be surprised if for a while you feel like you have never done strength training before. Nautilus is a unique muscular experience!

Why vary workouts at all? Very simply: to avoid mental and physical staleness. If you don't continually challenge yourself with new machines and new workouts, you'll find that old motivation slipping away.

Just as important, though, is the fact that everyone plateaus from time to time on certain machines. Physiological gains never accrue at an even pace. Don't be shocked if you progress smoothly from three to eight plates on the Women's Pullover, then spend the next 10 workouts at eight plates while everything else is increasing. As soon as you hit one of those plateaus, find an alternate exercise or just drop the machine for a while. As far as my colleagues and I know, *no one* has ever stopped progressing because he or she reached a personal physiological limit.

Ready? Let's start with a master list of body parts and the machines that can train them.

Body Part	*Nautilus Machine*
Buttocks (hip extensors, mainly the gluteus maximus and hamstrings)	Hip and Back Duo-Squat Leg Press on the Compound Leg machine
Front Thigh (quadriceps)	Leg Extension Leg Press Duo-Squat
Back Thigh (hamstrings)	Leg Curl Hip and Back Leg Press Duo-Squat
Inside/Outside Thigh (adductors/ abductors)	Adductor, Abductor Combination Ad/Ab
Calves (gastrocnemius, soleus)	Multiexercise Calf Raises
Hip Flexors (iliopsoas, rectus femoris of the quadriceps)	Hip Flexor
Lower Back (spinal erectors)	Lower Back Hip and Back
Upper Back (latissimus dorsi, teres major and minor, rhomboids, back deltoids)	Pullover/Torso-Arm Behind-Neck/Torso-Arm Multiexercise Chin-Ups Rowing Torso
Shoulders (front, middle, rear deltoids)	Double Shoulder 40-Degree Chest/Shoulder 70-Degree Shoulder Rowing Torso
Chest (pectoralis major and minor)	Double Chest Women's Chest Pullover 10-Degree Chest 40-Degree Chest/Shoulder

Body Part	*Nautilus Machine*
Upper Arms (biceps, triceps)	Multibiceps
	Multitriceps
	Plateloading Bi/Tri
	Multiexercise Triceps Dips
Forearms (flexors and extensors)	Multiexercise Wrist Curls and Reverse Wrist Curls
Midtorso (rectus abdominus, obliques, transverse abdominus	Abdominal
	Rotary Torso
	Multiexercise Side Bends
Neck (forward flexors, rear extensors, lateral flexors, rotators)	Four-Way Neck
	Rotary Neck
	Neck and Shoulder

SPECIFIC GUIDELINES FOR NEGATIVES

1. *Negative-only sets:* Try to lower to a count of 10–15. Follow these principles: When you can reverse the movement (lift yourself up) don't try to do it. When you can only hold yourself motionless, don't try. Try to stop the downward movement only after it becomes impossible to do so. This is another way of saying that for the first few negative-only reps you are strong enough to lift yourself back up or at least to stop the descent. You obviously don't want to do these things at this point, though. When you begin fatiguing, and you can no longer lift back up or stop yourself, fight to do so! End the set when you lose complete control over the lowering phase.

2. *Negative-accentuated sets:* On several machines you can move the weight into position with two arms or legs but do the negative phase with only one (Leg Extension, Leg Curl, for example). Follow the concepts outlined above for negative-only sets. Avoid negative-accentuated sets on machines that will lead to unnatural and dangerous postures, like the Pullover and the Neck and Shoulder.

3. *Negative-emphasized sets:* Use 20–30 percent *less* weight than with normal sets. The spotter will apply resistance on the negative phase. For example, you would perform a normal Incline Press on the Double Shoulder machine, but a spotter would push backward against the large foot pedal to add to the weight stack's resistance in the negative, or lowering, phase. Your spotter must be careful to apply force only in safe ranges of motion. Spotters must also be careful to avoid moving machine parts when applying resistance. *Never* touch a moving weight stack to add or subtract resistance.

4. Negative-only, negative-accentuated, and negative-emphasized sets may be interspersed throughout all your workouts once you have learned basic form and protocol.

5. Do not do all-negative workouts more than once a week. These are brutal if you really work at them, but they offer great results. Expect to be sore after your initial few negative sets and workouts. Prolonged, static stretching is the cure.

REVIEW OF WORKOUT GUIDELINES

1. Each workout should include no more than 12 exercises. The upper body is usually stressed, but athletes in running-oriented sports should do at least six lower-body machines.

2. The weight you choose should allow no more than 12 repetitions for the upper body exercises and 15 for the lower body.

3. The exercise should be terminated *only* when you've reached the point of momentary muscular failure. This *should* happen at 12 or 15 reps (upper or lower body), but if it doesn't, *keep going* until you cannot do another rep in good form.

4. Concentrate on flexibility by slowly letting the machines draw you into the stretched position.

5. Accentuate the lowering, or negative, phase of every

exercise by moving at one-half the speed with which you lifted the weight.

6. *Always move at a slow and controlled speed.* If ever in doubt about speed, move slower.

7. To maximize strength gains, rest for at least one minute between machines. To maximize cardiovascular benefits, move quickly between machines.

8. Once you can perform 12 (or 15) reps in good form, raise the weight 5 percent for your next workout. Use 1-, 2½-, and 5-pound weights, pinned to the weight stack, to add these small increments.

9. Train on Nautilus no more than three times a week. Allow at least 48 hours between workouts.

10. Keep accurate records of everything you do: date, reps, weight, negative variations, etc.

11. Do not do skill training for a sport right after a Nautilus workout. Make sure to rest for at least two hours between strength training and sport participation.

WORKOUTS

Beginner Workout 1

1. Hip and Back Machine
2. Leg Extension
3. Leg Press
4. Women's Pullover
5. Torso-Arm (either on Pullover/Torso-Arm or on single Torso-Arm machine)
6. Arm Cross (first movement on Double Chest or Women's Chest)
7. Incline Press (second movement on Double Chest; omit if not available)
8. Lateral Raise (first movement on Double Shoulder)
9. Overhead Press (second movement on Double Shoulder; negative-only if one plate cannot be raised at least five times)
10. Biceps Curl (Multibiceps or Plateloader)
11. Multiexercise Wrist Curls
12. Multiexercise Calf Raises

Beginner Workout 2

1. Hip and Back Machine
2. Leg Extension
3. Leg Curl
4. Behind-Neck (first movement on Behind-Neck/Torso-Arm combination, or the only movement on a Behind-Neck machine)
5. Torso Arm (either second movement or separate machine)
6. Rowing Torso
7. Multiexercise Triceps Dips (negative-only if fewer than five legal dips can be performed; weighted negatives if more than 10 can be performed)
8. Biceps Curl (Multibiceps or Plateloader)
9. Multiexercise Wrist Curls
10. Multiexercise Reverse Wrist Curls
11. Multiexercise Calf Raises

Beginner Workout 3

1. Leg Extension Machine
2. Duo-Squat
3. Leg Curl
4. Hip Adductor
5. Hip Abductor
6. Women's Pullover (or Men's if unavailable)
7. Multiexercise Chin-Ups (palms facing you, negative-only if fewer than five can be done in good form)
8. Women's Chest (or Arm Cross on Double Chest)
9. Incline Press (if exercise 8 was done on Double Chest; omit otherwise)
10. Biceps Curl (Multibiceps or Plateloader)
11. Multiexercise Wrist Curls
12. Four-Way Neck (all four directions)

Beginner Workout 4

1. Leg Extension
2. Duo-Squat
3. Leg Curl

4. Behind-Neck (on Combination Behind-Neck/Torso-Arm or on single unit)
5. Multiexercise Chin-Ups (see Beginner Workout 3)
6. Lateral Raise (first movement on Double Shoulder)
7. Overhead Press (second movement on Double Shoulder; negative-only if one plate cannot be raised five times)
8. Rowing Torso
9. Biceps Curl (Multibiceps or Plateloader)
10. Multiexercise Wrist Curls
11. Four-Way Neck (all four directions)
12. Multiexercise Calf Raises

Mixed Workout 1

1. Hip and Back Machine
2. Leg Extension
3. Leg Press (if Compound Leg is available)—negative-emphasized
4. Hip Adductor
5. Hip Abductor
6. Women's Pullover (or Men's if unavailable)
7. Torso Arm—negative-emphasized
8. Multiexercise Chin-Ups—negative-only (with weight belt if 10 good negatives can be performed)
9. Women's Chest (or Arm Cross on Double Chest)
10. Incline Press (if Women's unit unavailable)—negative-only
11 Multiexercise Triceps Dips
12. Biceps Curl—negative-emphasized

Mixed Workout 2

1. Women's Pullover (or Men's if unavailable)
2. Multiexercise Chin-Ups—negative-only (with weight belt if 10 good negatives can be performed)
3. Women's Chest (or Arm Cross on Double Chest)—negative-emphasized
4. Incline Press (if exercise 3 was done on Double Chest)—negative-emphasized

5. Lateral Raise (Double Shoulder)
6. Rowing Torso
7. Multiexercise Triceps Dips (negative-only if fewer than five legal Dips can be performed; weighted negatives if more than 10 negative-only can be performed)
8. Leg Extension—negative-assisted
9. Leg Curl—negative-emphasized
10. Multiexercise Calf Negatives—lift body plus weight stack (use belt) with the chin bar, lower with negative calf contraction

Mixed Workout 3

1. Duo-Squat Akinetic (set weight at 50–75 percent of standard load)
2. Leg Extension
3. Leg Press (if Compound Leg is available)—negative-emphasized
4. Hip Adductor
5. Hip Abductor
6. Women's Pullover (or Men's if unavailable)
7. Torso-Arm—negative-emphasized
8. Multiexercise Chin-Ups—negative-only (see Beginner Workout 3)
9. Women's Chest (or Arm Cross on Double Chest)
10. Biceps Curl—akinetic (if Multibiceps unit is available; set weight at 50–75 percent of normal load)
11. Triceps Extensions—akinetic (if Multitriceps unit is available; set weight at 50–75 percent of normal load)
12. Multiexercise Wrist Curls

Negative Workout 1

1. Leg Extension—negative-accentuated
2. Leg Press (if Compound Leg is available)—negative-emphasized
3. Leg Curl—negative-accentuated
4. Multiexercise Negative Calf (see Mixed Workout 2)
5. Women's Pullover (or Men's)—negative-only
6. Multiexercise Chin-Ups—negative-only

7. Lateral Raise (Double Shoulder)—negative-only
8. Overhead Press (Double Shoulder)—negative-only
9. Multiexercise Triceps Dips—negative-only
10. Biceps Curls—negative-accentuated

Negative Workout 2

1. Hip and Back Machine (normal)
2. Leg Extension—negative-emphasized
3. Leg Press (if Compound Leg is available)—negative-emphasized
4. Leg Curl—negative-only
5. Women's Pullover (or Men's)—negative-emphasized
6. Behind-Neck (normal)
7. Multiexercise Chin-Ups—negative-only (see Beginner Workout 3)
8. Overhead Press (Double Shoulder)—negative-only
9. Multiexercise Triceps Dips—negative-only (see Beginner Workout 2)
10. Biceps Curl—negative-only

Negative Workout 3

1. Women's Pullover (or Men's)
2. Multiexercise Chin-Ups—negative-only (see Mixed Workout 1)
3. Women's Chest (or Double Chest)—negative-emphasized
4. Incline Press (if exercise 3 was done on Double Shoulder)—negative-emphasized
5. Lateral Raise (Double Shoulder)
6. Rowing Torso
7. Multiexercise Triceps Dips—negative-only (see Beginner Workout 2)
8. Leg Extension—negative-accentuated
9. Leg Curl—negative-emphasized
10. Multiexercise Negative Calf Raises (see Mixed Workout 2)
11. Abdominal Machine

SPORT-SPECIFIC NAUTILUS TRAINING

The workouts listed above are, of course, a fraction of those possible to develop. If you compete on a serious basis in any recreational or varsity sport, you will want to maximize sport-related strength gains. Below you'll find some suggestions on particular machines or exercises to use for just about any sport you can play.

Basketball

Emphasize the legs! The Duo Squat and Compound Leg machines will be particularly helpful, though you need not use both; either will suffice. Forearms can be trained with Regular and Reverse Wrist Curls.

Photo courtesy of University of Texas Women's Athletics.

Bicycling

No surprises here—work your quads, hamstrings, and hip extensors on the leg machines. The forearms should be trained as well.

Bowling

Use the Double Shoulder for the deltoids, the Multibiceps and Multitriceps for the upper arms, and Regular and Reverse Wrist Curls.

Field Hockey

This is another sport that demands lower body work more than upper. *Do* work on deltoids, upper arms, and forearms. Latissimus not a priority.

Photo courtesy of University of Iowa Women's Athletics.

Golf

The rage of professional golf, Nautilus has established itself as a highly valuable training tool. Work on the Rotary Torso and Multiexercise Side Bends. Forearms, latissimus, and triceps should be trained as well.

Photo courtesy of University of Iowa Women's Athletics.

Gymnastics

No secrets here. This sport requires total-body muscular fitness. The all-around event requires more general training. If you specialize in one particular apparatus, discuss the major muscle groups with your coach and focus on them in strength work.

Photo courtesy of University of Iowa Women's Athletics.

Martial Arts

Suggestions depend on the branch and school that you are studying. Legs should always be stressed as they form your base of support.

Racquet Sports

Work the pectoralis (Chest machine), deltoids (Double Shoulder), biceps and triceps, and do both Regular and Reverse Wrist Curls.

Skating

Focus on the hip extensors (Duo-Squat, Compound Leg, Hip and Back) and the hip adductors and abductors.

Skiing

Alpine or downhill requires a slightly lesser focus on the upper body than does Nordic (cross-country). The latter is perhaps the most physiologically demanding of all sports and requires total-body muscular fitness. Don't neglect the Calf Raises, for the gastrocnemius is an important knee stabilizer.

Soccer

Again, no brains needed here to suggest placing a priority on lower-body work. Adductors and abductors should be included with quad, hamstring, and calf work.

Softball

Use the Double Shoulder, Women's or Double Chest, Biceps/Triceps, and Regular and Reverse Wrist Curls. Some fascinating research has recently shown how Nautilus training significantly increases throwing velocity for both pitchers and outfielders. Batting is also likely to be improved.

Photo courtesy of University of Iowa Women's Athletics.

Swimming

As in gymnastics, suggestions depend on stroke specialization. Breaststrokers need to emphasize the legs more than do swimmers of the other strokes. Adductors will be important here. All swimmers should focus on the latissimus (Pullover, Behind-Neck/Torso-Arm, Chins) and triceps. Biceps and deltoids are of lesser importance, though butterfliers should spend some time on the latter.

Photo courtesy of University of Texas Women's Athletics.

Tennis

Important machines are the Women's or Double Chest, the biceps and triceps units, and the Multiexercise for Regular and Reverse Wrist Curls.

Photo courtesy of University of Texas Women's Athletics.

Track/Running

This is another case of obvious leg focus. The Duo-Squat, Hip and Back, and Compound Leg are the most important

Photo courtesy of University of Texas Women's Athletics.

Photo courtesy of University of Texas Women's Athletics.

machines. Deltoids and upper arms should not be totally neglected, however.

Volleyball

Spikers will want to spend their time on the same basic three as the runners: Duo-Squat or Compound Leg and Hip and Back. The lower body in general deserves slightly greater emphasis than the upper body.

CHAPTER 9

DON'T FORGET AEROBIC EXERCISE

Whether it's to meet the demands of a tough set of tennis, a 10K run, a long day at work, or a household of kids, pets, vacuum cleaners, and washing machines, Nautilus will pay off. But it's *not* all there is.

As we discussed earlier, Nautilus gets four stars for muscular strength, but it's not a "perfect" form of exercise. Yes, flexibility is at least maintained and often enhanced. Yes, that mysterious quality called *metabolic endurance* is noticeably improved. And yes, the heart muscle is beating at a high percentage of its maximum for the duration of your workout. But Nautilus is *not* terribly aerobic. It's not a high calorie burner. It appears not to raise HDLs, the high-density lipoproteins that may reduce the risk of coronary artery disease.

If you're after total fitness and overall health enhancement, your 60 weekly Nautilus minutes should be augmented with aerobic exercise. Another 60 minutes squeezed in during the week may have significant effects on health, weight control, and aging, effects that Nautilus alone may not offer.

Four questions must be answered before you can head out along the aerobic trail:

- What types of exercise are aerobic and safe?
- How hard do I exercise?
- How long must I exercise?
- How often must I put myself through this?

For simplification, let's address these as type, intensity, duration, and frequency.

TYPES OF AEROBIC EXERCISE

Restating an earlier point, exercise is aerobic *only* if it involves large muscle groups, contracting rhythmically for at least 20 minutes, *and* a heart rate that is at least 60–70 percent of maximum. Here are your choices:

Careful strength training, stretching, and foot care make running a safe and effective aerobic choice. (Photo courtesy of University of Iowa Women's Athletics.)

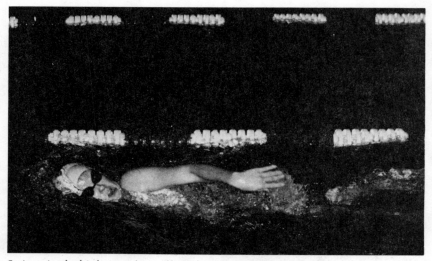

Swimming's high aerobic effect but low injury risk give it a top rating. (Photo courtesy of Patty Stewart, Rutgers University.)

Jogging/Running

This offers great benefits but at a high cost. It is a high calorie burner, it's inexpensive, it can be done anywhere with no equipment other than footwear, it raises HDLs, and it *significantly* slows several aspects of aging in the brains of rats that are experienced treadmill runners.

On the negative side, the orthopedic risks are great unless you keep mileage down, stretch and strength train properly, and get fitted properly for footwear. A number of noted orthopedic surgeons are on record stating that doing more than 50 miles per week may be a sure ticket to osteoarthritis at a later age.

Swimming

The benefits are great, the costs low, but it's tough to find a pool! This may be your best aerobic choice, for orthopedic risks are low but benefits are high. The difficulty lies in finding a 25-yard-or-longer pool to train in. Forget the 40-foot health spa pools—you'll never get your intensity high enough. (See sidebar.)

SWIMMING: A SEASON'S STRATEGY

Early Season Training

This is primarily LSD (long, slow distance). Fill your swim time with a few long, easy swims, broken up by some kicking drills. Break the boredom of overdistance training by varying breathing patterns and including some fartlek (speedplay) work. Utilize but don't overdo pulling drills (legs are buoyed and arms do all the work). Use all four strokes—freestyle, backstroke, breaststroke, and butterfly—but make sure at least 50 percent of your distance is free. (All distances given below are measured in yards.)

Early Season 60-Minute Workout

Warm-Up: 400 swim; 200 free, 200 breast
Swim: 1,000 free; first 500 breathe every four strokes, second
    500 every three
Kick: 400 individual medley; 100 each of fly, back, whip,
    flutter
Swim: 600 free; two laps easy, one lap hard

Mid-Season Training

This is primarily interval training with short rests. Get in at least two main sets per workout, with at least eight repeats of longer-than-race-distance swims and not more than 45 seconds of rest. If you compete at 200 yards, a sample set would be eight 300s. Concentrate on distance per stroke rather than on speed. Stretch out and still enjoy the swims. Make some sets all one stroke, some individual medley.

Mid-Season 60-Minute Workout

Warm-Up: 500 swim; 100 fly, 100 back, 100 breast, 200 free
Swim: 8 × 200 free, 30 seconds of rest, breathing every third
    stroke. Descending set: get progressively faster from #1 to
    #8 (inactive rest)
Kick: 8 × 100 flutter, 45 seconds of rest
Swim: 8 × 200 individual medley, 45 seconds of rest
Swim: Easy 200 cool-down

Late Season Training

You're still using interval training, but you'll swim fewer reps, with more rest, at faster speeds. This is the "up the quality, lower the quantity" phase of training. Keep thinking about technique, but speed is of the essence. Try "broken swims" to accustom your body to fast swimming (swim a 200, but rest for 10 seconds between 50s; this allows extrafast swimming).

Late Season 60-Minute Workout

Warm-Up: 300 swim; 100 kick, 200 swim (all freestyle)
Swim: 5 × 200, 60 seconds of rest (inactive), descending from
     #1 to #5, stroke of your choice
Kick: 4 × 100, 60 seconds of rest, flutter
Swim: 6 × 200 individual medley, 60 seconds rest, broken with
     10 seconds of rest at each 50 (inactive)
Swim: 500 easy, mixed strokes

Precompetition Swimming

Make sure your quantity of swimming and strength training is considerably reduced over the last three weeks before competition. Each workout should contain no more than 600 yards of hard swimming in the last week or two. Get plenty of sleep and eat well. Good luck!

Bicycling

This is another good choice given (1) a good exercise bike or road bike and (2) healthy knees. The big problem with cycling is that too many people jump on and pedal away without paying attention to intensity. Reading a magazine on the stationary bike is fine, but remember to keep your pulse in your aerobic training zone! (More on that below.)

The chance to read or watch television makes indoor cycling quite attractive. Keep the heart rate up! (Photo courtesy of Michaela McMillan.)

Rowing

This is a great aerobic choice, though it can be tough if your knees aren't healthy. Use a rower with a metronome not only to pace you but also to let you advance your workouts by stepping up stroke rate as you train.

Rowing has enjoyed a well-deserved surge in popularity in recent years. (Photo courtesy of Amerec, Inc.)

Jump Rope

Once you develop the ability to sustain jumping for 10 or more minutes it becomes a viable alternative. Build up to this by varying the "work-rest ratio"—start, for example, with 15 seconds of jumping and 45 seconds of rest. Progress to 15 work, 30 rest, then 15/15. You might then begin again with 30 seconds of jumping and 45 of rest and repeat the process. Do it gradually but always try to increase jumping time. (See sidebar.)

JUMPING ROPE THE INTERVAL WAY

Try this four-month plan for jumping rope through interval training.

Guidelines

1. Setting correct rope length: Stand on the middle of the rope—the handles should just reach your armpits. Tie knots near the handles to shorten the rope.
2. Keep the jumping height low, the knees flexible and slightly bent, and the wrists close to the body.
3. Jump at a rate of about 80 to 100 per minute.
4. Watch your pulse! Keep it *in* the training zone, not *above*.

Week	Jump Time	Rest Time	Repetitions	Daily Total
1	15 sec.	45 sec.	8	2 min.
2	15 sec.	30 sec.	12	3 min.
3	15 sec.	15 sec.	12	3 min.
4	30 sec.	30 sec.	8	4 min.
5	30 sec.	15 sec.	8	4 min.
6	45 sec.	20 sec.	8	6 min.
7	1 min.	30 sec.	7	7 min.
8	1.5 min.	30 sec.	6	9 min.
9	2 min.	1 min.	5	10 min.
10	2.5 min.	1 min.	5	12 min.
11	3 min.	1 min.	5	15 min.
12	4 min.	1 min.	4	16 min.
13	6 min.	1 min.	3	18 min.
14	7 min.	1 min.	3	21 min.
15	8 min.	1 min.	3	24 min.

Jump rope remains a great aerobic conditioner. (Photo courtesy of Bobby Hinds Lifeline.)

Minitrampolines/Rebounders

Beginners have trouble elevating their heart rates into their training zones, but this problem usually disappears with practice. These may be the next breakthrough in aerobic exercise, but the research isn't really in yet.

Minitrampolines or "Rebounders" reduce joint stress but allow high heart rates if used correctly. (Photo courtesy of Sundancer.)

Cross-Country Ski Simulators

This is one of my favorites. The simulators offer high aerobic benefit with almost zero orthopedic risk. There's good reason why the highest aerobic capacities ever recorded in man were found in elite cross-country skiers. (The average adult male can process 30–35 milliliters of oxygen, for every kilogram of his body weight, per minute. Elite Scandinavian Nordic skiers have been found to process up to *85* milliliters per kilogram per minute!)

Indoor Cross-Country (Nordic) skiing—on the most popular simulator. A great whole-body aerobic workout. (Photo courtesy of PSI, Inc.)

Properly conducted aerobic dancing offers great fun and aerobic benefit. Look for rhythmic and repetitive use of large muscles. (Photo courtesy of Jackie Rogers, Aerobics 'N Rhythm.)

Aerobic Dance

This is a tough one, for there are some good programs and some bad programs out there. Remembering that heart rate is *not* the sole factor in determining whether an exercise is aerobic, look for rhythmic movements of the large muscles, with intense dance segments of at least 15–20 minutes in duration. Without naming names, but to put you on guard, one of the nation's largest programs gets failing grades for its adherence to the principles of aerobic exercise. Beware!

INTENSITY OF EXERCISE

This is the component most often forgotten. The principle is simple: given the rhythmic involvement of large muscle groups, you must elevate the heart rate into the age- and fitness-related training zone. (How long to keep it there is next on the agenda.)

What is this training zone? Why isn't 100 percent again the goal? The zone is usually described as between 70 and 85 percent of your maximum heart rate. If you're at the very bottom of the fitness ladder, you'll start benefiting from exercise at 60 or 65 percent of max. You can measure heart rate with a wrist (radial) or neck (carotid) pulse, taken for 10 or 15 seconds and multiplied by six or four. Use two fingers and don't press too hard!

The good news is that very little additional benefit is gained by working out *above* 85–90 percent. For whatever reasons (and we're not sure of them yet), exercise in the 70–85 percent range is *plenty* hard enough for all those nice aerobic benefits. I wish we could say that for strength training!

Given the above, how do you establish your own training zone? Full, graded exercise stress tests are the best way to go, but these can cost more than $250. Many fitness centers administer submaximal, physical work capacity tests that predict maximum heart rate and aerobic condition. If these are both unavailable, you can approximate your training zone with the Karvonen formula:

$$[(220 \text{ minus AGE minus RESTING HEART RATE}) \times .70]$$
$$\text{plus RESTING HEART RATE}$$

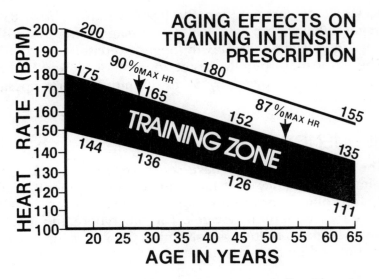

The zone one should train in decreases gradually with age.

Your resting heart rate should be taken several minutes after waking in the morning but before you get out of bed. Your target zone will be 10 beats on either side of the Karvonen number. For example:

Age: 25   Resting heart rate: 65

$$\text{KARVONEN NUMBER} = \left[(220 - 25 - 65) \times .70\right] + 65$$
$$= \left[\quad (130) \quad \times .70\right] + 65$$
$$= 91 + 65 = 156$$

TARGET ZONE $= 146 - 166$

After a five-minute warm-up, gradually elevate your pulse into this zone. Take your pulse every minute or so to check that you're working hard enough. Above the zone? Ease off. It's doing you no extra good and may force you to hit the showers early.

DURATION OF EXERCISE

Authorities have set the minimum duration of target heart rate zone exercise at 20 minutes, but the more, the merrier.

You *won't* get greater benefits from working above 85–90 percent of max, but you *will* see greater gains in aerobic fitness and weight control with *longer* exercise.

The 20-or-more-minute target zone phase should be both preceded and followed by 5- to 10-minute warm-ups and cool-downs.

FREQUENCY OF EXERCISE

These same authorities have set three days a week as the minimum frequency for significant training gains. If you're not overdoing things in terms of intensity, you can certainly do five days of aerobics a week. Too much here, though, and you will begin to reduce your Nautilus training gains. Set your priorities and go after them!

AEROBIC TRAINING TIPS

The key to avoiding aerobic boredom and keeping results coming at a steady pace is training variety. There are three basic ways to manipulate a given amount of aerobic work. They are:

- Long, slow distance (LSD) or Overdistance
- Interval training
- Fartlek or Speedplay

These three strategies apply to all eight aerobic exercises described above. Let's analyze them and include some training examples along the way.

Long, Slow Distance—LSD

This is the foundation of all aerobic training. You'll most often see athletes doing LSD at the beginning of the season. What they're doing is establishing a good aerobic base to which they can later add quality or speed training.

LSD has often been called *overdistance*, since it requires

that you train at distances far longer than those you might compete at. A 200-yard freestyler might, in the early season, swim a straight 2,000-yard freestyle at a slow pace. Similarly, a miler may limit her early season training to easy six- or eight-mile runs.

Suggestions for the aerobic eight described above? Some are amenable to LSD and some aren't, if you're just starting out. Cycling and perhaps rowing are two cases in which, as a novice, you can set a comfortable pace and last 20 minutes. Swimming and jogging are two cases in which you probably won't be ready for LSD for at least the first month of training. What do you do in that case? Read on.

Interval Training

Interval training probably is the major factor in the incredible drops in swimming and track world records in the last 30 years, and you can "do intervals" from day one of your training program.

Interval training, which I touched on briefly in the discussion of jumping rope, involves the manipulation of "work bouts" and "rest bouts." In English, this means you're going to alternate exercise and rest intervals. The relative timing of these two is called the *work-rest ratio*.

The reason that intervals are so effective is that the rest periods allow you to train with much higher quality, for much longer periods of time, before fatigue sets in. What happens chemically is that you never allow the level of lactic acid, muscle's waste product, to get so high that it forces you to quit. Neat trick!

Interval training can easily be structured to help the beginner or the elite athlete. Writing an interval training prescription, or ITP, is easy. The four components are:

- the number of repetitions;
- the distance or exercise time;
- the amount of rest between reps; and
- the type of rest between reps.

Taking swimming as an example, here's a common ITP:

[8 × 100 freestyle, 20 seconds of inactive rest]
- Swim 100 yards freestyle.
- Rest on the wall, keeping still, for 20 seconds.
- Repeat a total of eight times.

GUIDELINES FOR SETTING THE ITP

Number of Repetitions

A minimum of four should be done, and there is no practical maximum. Start low and increase gradually.

Distance or Exercise Time

A beginner should keep the duration very brief—as little as 15–30 seconds of work is fine to start with. There is no practical maximum for duration. One Saturday morning swim practice saw the coach give us 4 × 1,650 on 20 minutes. Talk about boredom! (On 20 minutes means that, rather than specify the amount of rest, we started a new 1,650 every 20 minutes. If we swam it in 18:30, we took 1:30 of rest.)

Amount of Rest

Beginners should strive to maximize total exercise time. This will probably require fairly long rest intervals. I taught a swim conditioning class at The University of Texas one summer that shows what high-rest interval training can do for the beginner. Five of the women who enrolled were nearly nonswimmers. They were able, on day one, to eke out 20 × 25 yards, freestyle, with one minute of rest. By the end of the week they managed 40 × 25 with a minute of rest. By the completion of the six-week course all five were swimming one-hour workouts of more than 2,200 yards!

If you're further along in training, you should start with high work-low rest ratios, then gradually increase the rest periods and the quality of the work periods. A sprinter might follow this plan:

Early season: High work-rest ratio; run 880, walk 110
Midseason: Medium work-rest ratio; run 440, walk 440
Late season: Low work-rest ratio; run 110, walk 880

Type of Rest between Reps

There are two types of rest: active and inactive.

Active rest involves light exercise in between reps or work bouts. A swimmer, for example, might swim an easy lap between those 100s. When do you use active, rather than inactive (or total) rest? It depends on what types of events you might be competing in and, therefore, which energy system you need to train.

The body has three basic energy systems (see Chapter 13 for more details):

- Stored phosphagens (ATP, CP)—responsible for the first 10 seconds of exercise
- Anaerobic system—primary responsibility for the first $1\frac{1}{2}$–2 minutes of exercise
- Aerobic system—in full swing by two minutes, responsible for long-term exercise

Here's the story on active versus inactive rest: if you remain totally inactive between reps, you give your stored phosphagen system time to recharge. This will let you do the next short rep at high speed. If you're a sprinter, you'll want to do lots of inactive-rest interval training.

If you stay slightly active between reps, you don't allow the stored phosphagens to replenish themselves. This will place extra stress on your anaerobic system. Athletes whose events are completed in from 45 seconds to three minutes will tend to do lots of active-rest intervals. If you're just starting your exercise program, you'll find it easier to use inactive rest between reps. The extra boost of phosphagens will keep you going a bit longer.

Fartlek or Speedplay

Scandinavian in origin, speedplay involves continuous exercise in which you alternate easy and hard intervals. A runner might, for example, in an eight-lap trip around a quarter-mile track, run the straights and walk the curves. A swimmer might alternate two hard laps with one easy one. Speedplay should last a minimum of 20 minutes.

THE BOTTOM LINE ON AEROBICS

Doing 20 minutes of aerobics, with the heart rate in the training zone and large muscles working rhythmically, is your goal. If you can't accomplish them at first, try interval training with a low work-rest ratio. Remember the swimmers at Texas! If 20 minutes in the training zone is no sweat (forgive the pun), add some spice with speedplay or harder intervals. If you're shooting for a competition, gradually increase the quality of the work and the length of the rest intervals. OK, you're ready. Get to it!

CHAPTER 10

LET'S EAT!

People are bombarded with and confused by nutritional information and misinformation from all sides. One government panel of 50 experts is likely to find their recommendations completely discredited by a second agency's panel of experts, and *both* panels are then attacked by the Meat, Dairy, and Poultry Councils. Who is one to believe?

This chapter is a synthesis of widely supported recommendations that you can start using from the moment you close the book. Good nutrition requires some work—both physical and mental. This chapter attacks the second part of that task, but it's up to you to go out and change your shopping and eating habits.

THE TRUTH ABOUT METABOLISM

Survival

Never forget one thing—our bodies have evolved into survival machines. Metabolic rate, or the amount of calories consumed in bodily functioning, is one of the variables most affected by dietary and exercise habits. *It is not fixed forever at any given level.* It can and does constantly shift, and you can take charge of it. All it takes is exercise and calorie control. That's right—no pills or drugs, just exercise and nutrition. Keep reading and the secrets will be revealed.

Basal Metabolic Rate

In calculating the number of calories you consume in a day, you start with a baseline known as the basal metabolic rate (BMR). This is the number of calories your body consumes in a totally resting state, after 12 hours without food or exercise. The BMR of adults ranges from 900 to 2,000 calories a day and is usually 10–15 percent higher in men because of their higher percentage of muscle.

Take note: Every pound of muscle you add to your body *raises your BMR.* In this regard, Nautilus training plays a significant but rarely noted role in weight control. If you are on a fat reduction program, strive to maintain muscle mass. A lean, muscular woman burns more calories just standing around than an obese woman does in light exercise! *Don't lose weight; lose fat.*

Adding the BMR to the calories spent in daily activities gives you your total daily expenditure. If this exceeds your daily caloric intake, you lose body weight. If it falls short of caloric intake, you gain weight.

Changing Your BMR

As I mentioned above, your BMR is not hopelessly fixed at some arbitrary point for the rest of your life. In fact, it's part of a complex survival system that adjusts and stabilizes you against changing environments. How does this mechanism work? Let's say you want to lose weight (fat), so you reduce your daily caloric intake from 2,200 to 1,000. Since you're burning 2,200 a day right now (1,500 calories a day BMR plus 700 activity), the drop to 1,000 would create a 1,200-calorie-per-day deficit. This should cause you to lose one pound every three days, right? Wrong. Your brain says, "The BMR is set at 1,500 because I need 1,500 calories a day to keep the show on the road. This clown is feeding me only 1,000. Keep this up and I'll have to start breaking things down. Survival is in jeopardy. I'll fix her—to keep things smooth, I'll just drop the BMR." BMR decreases, sometimes *drastically,* when you diet. Review this math exercise:

Old BMR: 1,500 calories; old activity: 700   TOTAL: 2,200 Cal
Caloric intake on diet: 1,000 calories   1,000 Cal
                              DAILY DEFICIT: 1,200 Cal
                              WEIGHT LOSS 3 *days:*   3,600 Cal
                                                             or 1 lb.

TWO WEEKS LATER (Give or take):

New BMR: 800 calories; activity level: 700   TOTAL: 1,500 Cal
Caloric intake on diet: 1,000 calories   1,000 Cal
                              DAILY DEFICIT: 500 Cal
                              WEIGHT LOSS 3 *days:*   1,500 Cal
                                                             or 7 oz.

So what happens? You're losing weight more slowly, you lose interest in the diet, and you return to your old eating habits.

Now consider this:

New BMR: 800 calories; activity level: 700   TOTAL: 1,500 Cal
Caloric intake: 2,200 calories   2,200 Cal
                              DAILY *SURPLUS:*   700 Cal
                              WEIGHT *GAIN* 5 days: 3,500 Cal
                                                             or 1 lb.

This is no short work of fiction. It's real, documented. It happens all the time. It's why *every* diet that doesn't cause permanent changes in exercise and eating habit *fails*. But gaining weight can be avoided.

There's really just one basic message here: Exercise every day. Eat well and follow guidelines. To lose fat, you need do nothing more than add 100–200 calories of exercise to your life *every day* and eat 100–200 fewer calories *every day.* Forget low-calorie reducing diets. Lifetime weight control can be accomplished only through daily exercise and smart eating.

THE ESSENTIAL NUTRIENTS

Carbohydrates

Carbohydrates are the major source of energy for the body's billions of cells. The carbohydrates in foods, whether in simple form such as in table sugar or honey or in complex form such as in potatoes or rice (starch), must eventually be broken down through digestion into simple sugar molecules. Sugar as glucose is then transported via the blood to cells throughout the body.

Glucose not being carried by the blood can be stored in the muscles and liver as chains called *glycogen*. The stored glycogen is sufficient for about 16 miles of running, averaging about 1,600 calories. Once glycogen storage has reached its peak, however, any excess glucose is converted into and stored as fat.

A dietary regimen known as *carbohydrate loading* has become popular as a means to cause the muscles to exceed their normal limits of glycogen storage. Briefly, the idea is first to empty the muscles of all stored glycogen (which is difficult and unpleasant), then to eat a very high percentage of complex carbohydrates in the two or three days prior to competition. For unknown reasons, the muscle supercompensates in many people after depletion and stores an unusually high amount of glycogen. While early research led thousands of endurance athletes to try carbo loading, later research was far from convincing. My advice? Skip it. The depletion process is difficult, and the reloading phase bloats you terribly because every gram of glycogen is stored with 2.7 grams of water. Adding one pound of glycogen to your body therefore adds almost three pounds of water. Stick to a high-carbohydrate diet (more on that below) and you'll be fine.

Fats

Fat is remarkably efficient in terms of its energy storage capabilities. In fact, one ounce of fat offers more than twice as much stored energy as an ounce of carbohydrate or protein. (The actual numbers are nine calories per gram of fat versus about four calories per gram of carbohydrate or protein.)

Unfortunately for those on fat reduction programs, fat is a key part of the survival mechanism—easy to store but tough to get rid of. In the old days (evolutionarily), when food wasn't always waiting on the dinner table, it made a lot of sense to have secure energy stores. After all, how many saber-toothed tigers can you chase down, kill, and eat in one week?

What you must never lose sight of in terms of fat reduction is that the body makes a very gradual shift from glycogen and blood glucose to fat during exercise. Estimates vary, but it appears that you don't make any real inroads into breakdown of stored fat until you've been exercising aerobically for at least 30 minutes. The best advice here is that fat reduction programs include exercise, on a daily basis, of moderate intensity but prolonged duration.

Just as Nautilus-induced muscle aids the dieter by raising the BMR, aerobic exercise such as running (1) keeps basal metabolism elevated for hours after exercise and (2) increases the body's ability to burn fat. Trained athletes are found to be far more efficient fat burners than nonathletes, and one major study with rats showed that treadmill-trained animals were 3.3 times more efficient in burning fat than sedentary control animals.

If an athlete working at a steady state suddenly starts to sprint, the body may have to revert to anaerobic processing and glucose/glycogen (see Chapter 13 for more details on this subject). It's obviously to the athlete's advantage to have as much glycogen left for the sprint (or just faster running) as possible, and that's one of the roles of fat. Since trained athletes can run quite well on stored fat, glycogen is spared for sprints and need not be used for steady state work. This is what is meant by the phrase *glycogen sparing*.

Protein

Chances are that if you're the average misguided athlete you can reduce your daily protein intake by 50 percent and still be consuming too much. Yes, protein is needed for maintenance, growth, and repair. But the amount you actually need is amazingly low. No reputable scientist *anywhere* has ever developed a shred of evidence that protein supplements are necessary for athletes, given moderate attention to diet.

The general guideline for protein intake is 0.9 grams per kilogram of body weight. With intense physical activity or during pregnancy this might rise to as high as 1.5 grams per kilogram. With a body weight of *110 pounds* or *50 kilograms,* and a recommended intake of *1.5 grams per kilogram,* for example, daily protein intake should be about *75 grams.*

What kinds of foods must you eat in one day to obtain 75 grams of protein? Are we talking about mountains of food? Thousands of calories? Pigging out on nine pounds of raw mountain lion meat? Hardly. How about six ounces of boneless chicken breast (300–350 calories) and three ounces of roast beef (165 calories). That's it. Now add to that what dairy products, vegetables, and grains contribute. Still going to waste time and money on protein powder? Give yourself a break.

Water—The Neglected Nutrient

Proper hydration, or water supply, is as important to the body as proper food intake. Without exception, every organ in the body functions in a watery medium. Depletion of body water leads to severe physiological disruption and eventual death. Because of the bullheadedness of a few coaches, about five high school and college athletes die each year from heat stroke after being denied water during workouts. This outdated and deadly practice continues in certain places to this day and must be stopped whenever detected.

How much water is required for proper hydration? Should you use commercial preparations such as Gatorade? The research is fairly clear on one conclusion: drink before a contest, during a contest, and after a contest. What to drink? Water, plain and simple. There is no hard evidence that any

GUIDELINES FOR ELECTROLYTE AND FLUID REPLACEMENT

Forget commercial hype—the following guidelines are based on solid, scientific research, and were drawn up by four sports nutritionists.*

- To promote rapid absorption of fluid, beverages should contain, per quart, less than 25 grams of carbohydrate (two tablespoons of sugar), less than 230 milligrams of sodium (one-tenth teaspoon of table salt), and less than 195 milligrams of potassium. They should contain *no* protein or fat. Best temperature for absorption is 45–55°F.
- *Before exercise:* drink about 16 ounces of water 10–15 minutes beforehand.
- *During exercise:* drink four to six ounces of water at 10-minute intervals.
- *After exercise:* replace each pound of water lost with 16 ounces of water or the beverages listed below.
- *Master list of beverages for fluid replacement:* dilute commercial preparations as instructed below. Most are far too concentrated, according to researchers.
  Water: Use as is. The *number one* choice.
  Body Punch: 1 part Body Punch, 1 part water
  E.R.G.: 1 part E.R.G.; 1 part water
  Bike Half-Time Punch: 1 part Bike Half-Time Punch; 2 parts water
  Gatorade: 1 part Gatorade; 2 parts water
  Quick Kick: 1 part Quick Kick; 2 parts water
  Sportade: 1 part Sportade; 3 parts water
  Take 5: 1 part Take 5; 7 parts water
  Fruit Juices: 1 part juice; 7 parts water
  Club Soda: Use as is if defizzed for before/during use
  Perrier: Use as is if defizzed for before/during use
  Diet Sodas: 1 part diet soda; 1 part water; defizz if for before or during exercise use
  Sweetened Sodas: 1 part soda; 3 parts water; defizz if used before or during exercise
- *Avoid or use with caution:* Alcohol and caffeine. Both promote urination and can be dehydrating; individual reactions vary widely.
- *Avoid completely:* Salt tablets. They interfere with fluid absorption, aggravate dehydration, and can cause nausea and stomach distress.

*From: *A Guide for Rapid Fluid and Safe Salt Replacement in Exercise.* Merle Best, Diana Galandak, Marilyn Schorin, and Frances Trakis-Fisher. Produced by EIC-NW, Morris Plains, NJ, 1982.

of the athletic drinks do more for you than water and no evidence that your body can't restore electrolyte balance without outside help. How much to drink? Before exercise in the heat, drink about 13–20 ounces of cold water. Yes, cold. Cold water is absorbed much faster than warm. During exercise in the heat, drink about four to six ounces every 10–15 minutes. Remember that the stomach can process only about 26 ounces of fluid per hour. Drinking more than that will leave you with fluid sloshing around in your stomach.

Gastric emptying is slowed by sugar in fluid. If you won't stick to cold water, follow the guidelines in the chart on how to dilute overconcentrated commercial drinks.

Vitamins and Minerals

Even if you have good eating habits, here you may be in trouble. So much of the vitamin and mineral content of foods is lost in transport, storage, and preparation that, unless you buy fresh and prepare correctly and quickly, you may need a commercial supplement. I'm a firm believer in obtaining nutrients from foods instead of bottles, but it's tough for many people.

Women have several special considerations here:

- Menstruation is an obvious time for increased iron intake. Foods to choose from include liver and kidney, dried fruits, oysters and shellfish, and leafy green vegetables.
- Calcium intake, discussed in the next chapter as well, must be maintained to prevent osteoporosis, the loss of mineral content from bone.
- Pregnant and lactating women must increase their intake of several nutrients, especially calcium, iron, folacin, and vitamin A. Milk should be stressed as the primary dairy product, for B vitamins, magnesium, and potassium are lost in the whey when cheese is made.
- Women taking birth control pills need to increase their intake of vitamin B_6 and folacin. For B_6, choose wisely from the whole-grain breads and cereals; enriched white

flour does *not* contain the B_6 lost in refining. Extra folacin can be obtained through daily servings of dark leafy vegetables and one serving of liver a week.

YOUR DAILY STRATEGY

The following plan is based on the National Academy of Sciences' report on diet, nutrition, and cancer. While the subject of some controversy, it is in my opinion the best advice to follow. Since one day's menu contains about 1,800 calories, you will need to adjust intake as necessary for your needs.

Fruits and Vegetables

Eat six or more daily servings of fruits and vegetables. A serving is one piece of fresh fruit or ½ cup frozen, raw, or cooked vegetables.

Fruits and vegetables high in vitamin C and/or A: mango, papaya, cantaloupe, watermelon, strawberries, citrus fruits, broccoli, spinach, kale, escarole, romaine lettuce, parsley, peppers, cabbage, white potatoes, sweet potatoes, carrots, acorn squash, butternut squash, and Brussels sprouts.

Of the recommended cruciferous vegetables—broccoli, Brussels sprouts, kale, cabbage, and cauliflower—only cauliflower is not high in vitamin A or C.

Whole Grains and Cereals

Eat five servings of whole grains. Two slices of bread, two muffins, or ½ cup of cooked cereal equals one serving.

Whole-grain products include whole-wheat bread, brown rice, corn and cornmeal, wheat germ, bran, barley, buckwheat groats, bulgur, and oatmeal.

Protein-Rich Foods

Eat two to three servings of low-fat dairy products, lean fish, meat, poultry, eggs, beans, or nuts. A cup of skim milk, 1½

SEVEN DIETARY GUIDELINES FOR AMERICANS* (THE U.S. DEPARTMENTS OF AGRICULTURE AND HEALTH AND HUMAN SERVICES)

1. *Eat a variety of foods.* Selections should include fruits; vegetables; whole-grain and enriched breads, cereals, and grain products; milk, cheese, and yogurt; meats, poultry, fish, eggs; and legumes.
2. *Maintain ideal weight.* Best established through body composition assessment rather than height-weight-frame charts. Eat slowly; prepare smaller portions; avoid seconds; increase physical activity; eat less fat and fatty foods; eat less sugar and sweets; avoid too much alcohol.
3. *Avoid too much fat, saturated fat, and cholesterol.* Choose lean meats, fish, poultry, dry beans and peas as your protein meat sources; moderate your use of eggs and organ meats like liver; trim excess fat where possible; bake, broil, or boil rather than fry; limit intake of butter, cream, hydrogenated margarines, shortenings, and coconut oil; read labels.
4. *Eat foods with adequate starch and fiber.* Substitute starches for sugars and fats; select foods such as whole-grain breads and cereals, fruits and vegetables, beans, peas, and nuts.
5. *Avoid too much sugar.* Use less of all sugars, including white, brown, raw versions, honey, and syrups; eat less of foods containing these sugars; select fresh fruits or canned-in-own-juices fruits; read labels for hidden sugars like sucrose, glucose, maltose, dextrose, lactose, or fructose.
6. *Avoid too much sodium.* Learn to enjoy the unsalted flavors of foods; cook with only small amounts of added salt; add little or no salt to foods at the table; limit intake of salty foods such as pretzels, potato chips, condiments (soy sauce, for example), cheese, cured meats, and pickled items; read food labels carefully to find all sources (sodium bicarbonate, for example).
7. *If you drink alcohol, do so in moderation.* These beverages tend to be very high in calories but very low in nutrients. Drinking can interfere with the absorption of important nutrients and has been linked to birth defects in the children of drinking mothers.

*From USDA Home and Garden Bulletin No. 232, *Nutrition and Your Health: Dietary Guidelines for Americans.*

ounces of cheese, or a cup of low-fat yogurt equals one serving.

Dairy products high in fat are whole-milk products, cream, most cheeses (harder cheeses are better than soft), ice cream, and sour cream.

Two or three ounces of boneless fish, meat, or poultry or one egg equals one serving. Trim exterior fat from meat; choose meat with little marbling; eat white meat chicken and turkey and remove skin.

Up to a cup of cooked beans or $\frac{1}{4}$ cup of nuts equals one serving. The dried-beans category includes lentils, dried peas, and chickpeas. Nuts are high in fat.

Occasional Inclusions

In addition to oil, butter, and margarine, foods high in fat include mayonnaise, salad dressing, rich desserts, and fried and creamed foods.

TIPS ON FOOD SELECTION, STORAGE, AND COOKING

- Carbohydrates, primarily the complex forms, *must* be stressed. At least 60 percent of daily calories must come from this group.
- Protein is generally overconsumed. Protein calories should comprise about 10–15 percent of daily calories. Use the guidelines of 0.9–1.5 grams per kilogram.
- One serving of liver per week will give you a two-week supply of vitamin B_{12}, a 10-day supply of vitamin A, a two-day supply of riboflavin, and 12 percent of your daily iron needs.
- Lean meats, skinless poultry, and low-fat dairy products offer more nutrients per calorie than their fattier versions and may reduce the risk of diet-induced cancer.
- Whole grains (whole-wheat pasta, oatmeal, brown rice) have more nutrients than foods made from refined (even if enriched) grains.
- Dark green leafy vegetables and deep yellow vegetables have more vitamin A than lighter-colored ones.

- Fresh or frozen fruits and vegetables are more nutrient-packed than canned ones. If fresh foods have been long in transit or storage, the frozen type might be more nutritious.
- Look for produce that has been kept cold in the store. This reduces the effect of nutrient-destroying enzymes.
- Fruits ripened on the plant and in the sun have more vitamin C than those picked green. Outdoor-grown tomatoes have twice the vitamin C of greenhouse versions.
- Ripe fruits and vegetables should be stored cold until eaten to reduce nutrient loss.
- Potatoes, canned foods, and grain foods should be stored in a cool, dark, and dry place. Don't refrigerate potatoes.
- Milk and bread should be kept in opaque containers to prevent destruction of riboflavin and vitamins A and D.
- Wash produce quickly, for soaking can rinse away water-soluble vitamins and minerals.
- Refrigerate all cooked foods that are not going to be eaten immediately.
- Keep fresh, cut, and cooked foods well-wrapped to reduce exposure to air.
- Waterless cooking, pressure cooking, steaming, stir-frying, and microwaving are least destructive of nutrients.
- Reduce cooking time as well as the surface area of food exposed during cooking whenever possible.

Bon appetít!

CHAPTER 11

SPECIAL CONSIDERATIONS FOR THE EXERCISING WOMAN

What about exercise during pregnancy? Menstruation? Effects on varicose veins? This chapter is devoted to answering some specific questions that exercising women ask.

Q. *Is it safe to exercise during pregnancy?*
A. Given proper supervision, which is always in order, the answer is an unqualified yes. Research data are piling up to support the fact that correctly performed and supervised exercise during pregnancy is far more than safe. It appears to ease delivery, reduce complications of labor and delivery, and speed the return to postpartum physical fitness.

Q. *Won't Nautilus training put too great a stress on my body?*
A. Again, not when performed and monitored correctly. The pioneer in this area is Dr. Doug Hall, an obstetrician-gynecologist in Ocala, Florida. He and his associates run a facility where more than 200 women train for their pregnancy on Nautilus equipment, treadmills, and exercise bicycles. Results have surpassed already-high expectations.

Q. *What guidelines should I follow for exercise during pregnancy?*
A. It depends on whether or not you were a habitual exerciser before you got the good news. If you were, you may continue at that level of intensity as long as the pregnancy

runs a normal and healthy course. If you weren't, you must start at a very low level and progress at a slow pace. In either case, fatigue, heart rates above 70–75 percent of max, and hyperthermia (high temperatures) should be avoided. Always watch your pulse rate!

According to Dr. Mona Shangold, noted sports gynecologist, the following warning signs are cause for immediate evaluation and the cessation of training: pain, bleeding, rupture of membranes, or absence of fetal movement. Exercise may be resumed *only* on doctor's advice.

Some problems have been noted with heavy exercise during the third trimester, and runners may be showing a higher rate of Caesarean section than other exercising mothers. *Always check with your doctor.*

Q. *What types of exercise will help me most during labor and delivery?*

A. Childbirth can be the most awesome physical challenge that any human being can face. The experiences of Dr. Hall's Nautilus-trained mothers-to-be suggest that strength and cardiovascular training are the keys to facing the challenge.

The four major areas for strength training are the abdomen, back, legs, and chest. Since labor can sometimes turn into an aerobic ordeal, don't forget low-trauma aerobic options like swimming, stationary cycling, and rowing.

Nautilus machines for the pregnant woman:

Lower Back machine (Use a spotter to get in and out)
Abdominal machine
Hip and Back machine
Leg Extension machine
Hip Adductor *and* Abductor
Behind-Neck machine
Women's Chest or Double Chest

Q. *What effects will exercise have on menstrual bleeding and cramps?*

A. Many women report that regular exercise helps relieve menstrual discomfort, and there are no known reasons to avoid exercise during this phase of the cycle. In fact, detailed research shows that women have set world records and won Olympic gold medals during *all* phases of the menstrual cycle.

Heavy menstrual cramps often respond well to a new class of drugs known as *prostaglandin inhibitors*. Ask your doctor about them.

Q. *Has exercise been linked to menstrual irregularity or disappearance?*

A. Concern has grown in the last few years over the fact that so many athletic women are experiencing amenorrhea (complete cessation of menstruation) or oligomenorrhea (irregular menstruation). It appeared for a time that low body fat was the key cause.

Researchers are now fairly well convinced that it is the overall stress of athletics and training, and *not* low body fat by itself, that leads to the problems. Sports gynecologists recommend that women past expected menarche who are not experiencing normal cycles see a doctor. Since no one knows the long-term effects, if any, of amenorrhea or oligomenorrhea, don't take any chances by diagnosing yourself.

Q. *What effects does exercise have on varicose veins?*

A. Exercise may be your best hope in preventing or reducing varicose veins. Besides doing some form of daily aerobic exercise (brisk walking is great), you should avoid standing for long time periods, wear support hose, and keep your feet elevated when sitting. Strength training's effects are unknown but expected to be beneficial.

Q. *After reading through this text, I'd like to know where all those Nautilus instructors got the idea that Nautilus builds strength without bulk, while barbells build strength and bulk.*

A. I'm glad you asked that question! I wish I knew the answer so I could do something about it. The only factor that determines bulk development is the presence or absence of male sex hormones. Whether you are a man or a woman, you will respond to high intensity strength training, barbell *or* Nautilus, with muscle hypertrophy (growth) only if the male hormones are present. Most women show great gains in strength with *no* addition of bulk due to their relative lack of testosterone.

Q. *I've heard a great deal lately about women and osteoporosis. What role does exercise play?*
A. Osteoporosis is the gradual loss of mineral content—and therefore strength—of bone with aging. It is most apparent and significant in women and can be seen as early as the late 20s and early 30s.

Regular exercise plays a *major* role in reducing or eliminating mineral loss from bone. One recent study compared a group of women runners (15 miles per week minimum) with a matched group of sedentary women. Not only had the runners shown no loss of mineral content but most *exceeded* the norms for their ages!

Researchers have yet to determine if strength training can have the same effect. Opinion is leaning strongly toward a "yes." Remember also to maintain calcium intake, either naturally or through supplementation. Again, see your doctor.

Q. *Many claims have been made about strength training's effects on the bustline. What's your opinion?*
A. There's a two-part answer. First, the breasts themselves contain no muscle tissue connected to underlying structures. Exercises for the pectoralis muscles can help to some degree, for they do play a supporting role. Don't expect miracles from strength training alone if a significant bustline problem already exists.

Second, exercise and caloric deficit can lead to fat loss from the breasts and therefore a reduction in size. Combine strength work and fat loss and you should see some benefits of firming and uplifting of the breasts.

Q. *Will we ever see a woman world record holder beat a man at his sport? What are the male-female differences that bear on the battle between the sexes?*

A. There are three areas that we can look at in answering this question. Based on sex differences in (1) anatomy, (2) cardiovascular systems, and (3) strength and power, we'll conclude that some sports are ripe for intersex competition, while others will never be.

ANATOMICAL DIFFERENCES

There are several important sex differences that bear heavily on head-to-head competition in the athletic arena. Perhaps the most important of these is body fat. Independent of whether you're world class or sedentary, you'll have at least 8 percent more fat on your body than a comparably fit man. For a 125-pound woman, that means carrying 10 pounds of extra baggage.

Body fat is present in two forms. Storage fat forms an insulating layer just below the skin and a protective sheath around internal organs. It acts as the body's nutritional reserve and is burned to provide energy during exercise. Males in their 20s carry about 12 percent of their body weight as storage fat. Women of the same age carry a fairly similar 15 percent of their weight as storage fat.

The big sex difference, however, is in essential fat. Essential fat is stored throughout the body's internal organs and is required for normal physiological functioning. While men have only about 3 percent essential fat, women are hormonally programmed to carry about four times as much, or 12 percent.

Adding up the two components, we see that college-aged men average about 15 percent fat, while the female counterpart carries 27 percent. Storage fat in both sexes can be reduced through training, but a gap always remains. While men can get as low as 3 percent, women rarely are found in good health with body fat below 8–10 percent. This is simply extra weight that takes a toll in any sport where the body must be propelled across or above land.

In at least one sport, however, this difference is to women's advantage. In an aquatic environment the woman's greater essential fat gives her some marked advantages. Fat has a lower density than water and therefore floats. Due to her higher fat storage, the average woman is usually 10 percent more buoyant than the average male. Also, the fact that the woman's greater fat is largely deposited in her upper legs improves her streamlining. These two circumstances translate into an amazing figure: women can actually swim any given distance at a 20–30 percent *lower* energy cost than a man of the same size!

This also means that women can achieve higher speeds than men at any given level of energy expenditure. At longer distances, where sheer strength is less important than endurance and efficient use of muscular energy, the gap between men and women decreases. Given the trend of the past 10 years, men and women 1,500-meter swimmers may be in the same heats by the year 1990.

CARDIOVASCULAR DIFFERENCES

Women just don't have as much heart as men do! In the physiological sense it's true. Women suffer from some severe limitations in comparison with similarly sized men, including:

- smaller heart size
- smaller total blood volume
- smaller total hemoglobin (oxygen-carrying compound found in blood)
- lower oxygen pulse (oxygen that can be processed per heartbeat)

On the surface these factors appear to explain why women have a 15–25 percent lower maximum oxygen uptake, or MAX $\dot{V}O_2$, than men. This is the ability of the muscles to extract oxygen from the blood and is described as milliliters of oxygen, per kilogram of body weight, per minute. MAX $\dot{V}O_2$ can go as high as 85 ml/kg/min in elite male Nordic (cross-country) skiers. A healthy college-aged woman will have a MAX $\dot{V}O_2$ of 35–45 ml/kg/min; a man 42–54 ml/kg/min. This 15–25 percent difference suggests that women may be fully one-quarter less efficient in getting oxygen to their muscles.

But what about the woman's greater fat percentage? Doesn't that affect cardiovascular efficiency? It very definitely does. Researchers have shown that sex differences in cardiac output and oxygen delivery nearly disappear when differences in fat percentage are accounted for. Similarly, a number of scientists have shown that when you express MAX $\dot{V}O_2$ as a function of a person's lean body weight (everything but fat), sex differences drop to as little as 10 percent.

Don't arrange a battle of the sexes just yet, though. Most sports require that you carry your body from one place to another, and there's little real value in statistically removing your extra body fat. The handicap will still be there.

STRENGTH AND POWER DIFFERENCES

When men and women of the same height are compared anatomically, the man will generally have more massive bones, larger joints with correspondingly larger articular surfaces (where bones meet and slide), and longer arm and leg segments. These differences translate biomechanically into greater leverage for the male skeleton. Were muscular strength alone to be equalized, this greater leverage would still enable the man to move his limbs with greater force and/or velocity than the woman.

It will come as no surprise that a woman's strength is generally two-thirds that of a similarly sized man. It *will* probably surprise you, though, that when leg strength is measured in terms of lean body weight (eliminating the fat statistically again), women show greater strength than men! Alas, this is once again nice but not meaningful. Women long jumpers and high jumpers may equal male jumpers in strength per unit of lean body mass, but they still have to move that extra body fat over the bar or out into the pit. Sex comparisons in these two events show the widest gaps of any.

Underlying the equality in strength, if fat is statistically eliminated, are the following facts.

- There is no sex difference in individual muscle fibers. Male and female fibers of identical size have identical contraction properties.

- There is little or no sex difference in relative muscle storage of the important quick fuels—ATP and creatine phosphate, and glycogen.
- There is no evidence of any sex difference in percent strength gains with weight training.

There are two qualifying factors, though. First, since men have as much as 20–30 times more testosterone (the male sex hormone) than women, they show much greater muscular *growth* in response to training. This phenomenon of equal *percentage* gains in strength without the *size* gains males show may reflect greater neural efficiency in women when strength training.

These differences in testosterone levels largely explain why it is a rare woman who develops bulging muscles from weight training. Testosterone is the chemical compound that plays a dominant role in guiding the development of the so-called sex characteristics. It is this compound that gives men their facial hair, their deeper voices, and their larger bones. While the exact mechanisms by which testosterone works are yet to be understood, its effects are clear: more testosterone enables greater assimilation of protein and the resulting greater ability of men to build muscle.

Why, then, wouldn't a woman interested in muscle mass want to take testosterone to narrow this sex difference? It is precisely those sex characteristics noted above that answer the question, for they begin to appear when female testosterone levels rise. Some of the "bearded ladies" populating our nation's circuses are true examples of these effects. There was in fact quite a furor over the explosion of the East German women onto the international swimming scene several years back, with accusations made of just such sex hormone doping (*anabolic steroids* is the term you've probably heard). The sometimes deeper voices, larger bone structures, and apparently abnormal muscular growth were quickly ascribed to drug intervention, but the charges have never been irrefutably substantiated. Our country's experience with plain old strength training for women, which the East Germans stimulated, has led many to conclude that the East Germans were simply finding and training the biggest and strongest women they could get.

The second qualifying factor is *total* storage of fuel sources. Yes, men and women have equal fuel storage per given amount of muscle, but since men have *greater* total muscle mass, they also have greater total fuel stores. This gives men the advantage in sports requiring quick surges of energy, such as sprinting.

In summary, women have a long and glorious road ahead in the skill sports, where anatomy and strength/power aren't as critical, and in swimming, where their added buoyancy makes them more efficient. It looks, though, like the sexes will never compete on an equal basis anytime the body must be transported across or off the ground. Does this matter? No! There's only one battle that counts in life, and that's the one in which you face yourself: the fears, the doubts, the pain, the sweat. But once you wage that battle and win, you'll be on top and in control. Nautilus is the battleground. I hope that I've given you the right strategy for the conflict and I wish you luck!

CHAPTER 12

NAUTILUS: HOW IT ALL WORKS

An overloaded muscle will grow. It's that simple. At any *one* point in a contraction, the muscle truly doesn't know or care how it is being overloaded. It's an illogical and incorrect jump, however, to the statement that all modes of strength training are alike. The Nautilus system is based on a number of principles—in part research-supported, in part only intuitive—that distinguish it from all others.

What are these principles? What can a Nautilus training program do for you? Let's analyze the Nautilus system a step at a time.

NAUTILUS: WHAT IT IS

Variable Resistance

The overload principle—probably the most important tenet of strength training—states that the stimulus for the growth of muscle is loading at some fairly high percentage of ability. If you could easily lift an 80-pound barbell 20 times, *no* number of 10-pound barbell lifts would make those muscles grow. Unfortunately, we know few of the precise details on just what percentage of maximum muscular force or strength you should train at, how many lifts or repetitions you should perform, and how many sets of repetitions are optimal. We've got some great clues, but nothing is written in stone.

While what little research that's been done suggests the necessity of two or three sets of 8–12 repetitions at about 75 percent of max, there may be a better way. Through the 12 years of its existence, the Nautilus system has been convincing tens of thousands of users, from pro football players to world-renowned ballerinas to housewives, that "one set taken to muscular failure" is enough. And the major reason that one set may be all you need is the Nautilus approach to variable resistance.

A given muscle does not have one particular, identifiable strength. Because the muscle itself is extremely complicated in structure, and because its physical relations with the bones it's moving are always changing, your strength actually changes as you move. This strength, or force value, can be measured at each point in a range of motion. Let's take a Biceps Curl as an example. Stand up and place your right arm by your side with palm out. Slowly lift the lower arm while keeping the elbow by your side. As you measure your strength, you might find that:

- you can exert 10 pounds of force with your palm at the leg;
- you can exert 25 pounds after rotating your palm up 45-degrees;
- you can exert 38 pounds with your forearm parallel to the floor;
- you can exert 21 pounds after 45-degrees more rotation toward the shoulder;
- with your palm at your shoulder you can create 12 pounds of force.

If you were to plot this graphically, you would have a strength curve, or your ability to create force at each point through the range of motion. It *always* changes, for *every* muscle. And every muscle changes in a different way. Some, like the elbow flexors (the biceps and brachialis), show a weak-strong-weak curve as they contract. Some, like the hamstrings in the back of your thigh, start out quite strong but show almost a straight decline in force as they contract.

OK, enough biomechanics. How does this affect you? Since your muscle's strength changes as it contracts, proper and maximal strength training demands a similarly changing bar-

MATCHING THE CAM TO YOUR STRENGTH CURVE

CAM	RADIUS (inches)	WEIGHT (pounds)	EFFECTIVE RESISTANCE (inch-pounds)
1.	6.5	30	195
2.	7.5	30	225
3.	6.5	30	195
4.	5.0	30	150
5.	4.0	30	120

Numbers 1–5 on the cam refer to the changing radius. The weight stack always equals 30 pounds, but the cam changes the load on your muscles by changing its radius.

THE BICEPS CURL: EFFECTIVE RESISTANCE WITH A 30 POUND BARBELL

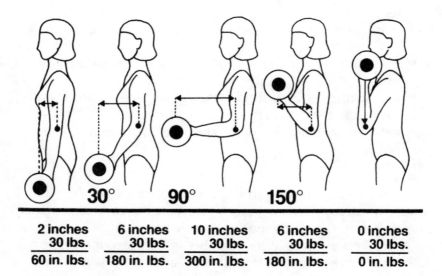

30°	90°	150°		
2 inches	6 inches	10 inches	6 inches	0 inches
30 lbs.	30 lbs.	30 lbs.	30 lbs.	30 lbs.
60 in. lbs.	180 in. lbs.	300 in. lbs.	180 in. lbs.	0 in. lbs.

The "effective resistance" of a 30-pound barbell changes according to the laws of physics. The load your muscles feel is obtained by multiplying the barbell weight by the "moment arm," or the horizontal arrows.

bell. If you can move only 10 pounds at the start of the Curl, and I give you a 35-pound barbell, you will not be able to move it. If you then resort to training with a 10-pound barbell, what happens at midrange when your muscles can create 38 pounds of force? No overload and no strength gain.

Enter the cam. What Nautilus has done is to give you an intelligent barbell that changes as your muscles change. By taking a fixed amount of weight, but directing its lifting chain around an oddly and uniquely shaped cam, Nautilus pulls off the trick—making one load of 40 pounds seem like 20 at one point and 50 at another. Given this increased efficiency of training, one set of repetitions rather than three may be all you need.

Direct Resistance

It would be nice if you could just apply the training resistance right where the muscle attaches. Take that Biceps Curl again. The elbow flexors attach to the forearm just below the elbow, but to train them, the resistance must be placed down at the hands. Fortunately, your forearms are strong enough so that your hands can hold a heavy weight long enough for sufficient overloading of the biceps. This is not always the case, though.

Case in point: the latissimus dorsi of the back. This large muscle fans up and out from the midline of the back and attaches to the upper arm. The lats can either pull the arms down with great force or, if the arms are fixed, pull the body up. Historically one of the best ways to train your lats has been to do Chin-Ups. These work extremely well but still suffer from the problem that when your hands lose their grip the exercise ends. If your lats are not strong enough for you even to *do* Chin-Ups, this is not a big deal. As soon as you develop lat strength, however, your forearms will fail *before* your lats do. And you will not have sufficiently overloaded them. Result: less than maximal efficiency.

What Nautilus attempts to do is apply the resistance as closely as possible to the point where the muscles being trained attach. The Pullover machine does this well—you apply force with your elbows, fairly close to where the lats attach—and grip strength is of no consequence. Where possible, Nautilus has incorporated direct resistance into its machines.

Rotary Movement

Human movement is accomplished through rotation. Sometimes, as in the case of the hand's path in a Biceps Curl, movement is purely rotational. At other times, combining rotation at two or more joints can yield straight-line action. Place both hands at your shoulders and press them overhead. Through a combination of rotation at the shoulder and elbow, the hands move in a straight line.

For strength training to be maximally efficient, the resistance or overload should match the movement being trained. Most strength-training equipment, Nautilus included, uses rotary resistance wherever possible.

Positive and Negative Work

Muscles, as you know, contract actively but cannot lengthen actively. Human extension and pushing movements are accomplished simply by using muscles in pairs. These are called *agonist-antagonist pairs*. The elbow flexors contract to bring the palm up toward the shoulder. Call them the *agonists*. The triceps, or elbow extensors on the back of the arm, contract to extend the arm back from flexion. They are the *antagonists*.

What you may not have realized, though, is that the same muscle that lifts a weight is responsible for lowering it against gravity's pull. The elbow flexors not only lift the weight in the curl movement; they lower it as well.

A contraction in which a resistance is lifted against gravity and the muscle shortens is called *concentric* or *positive work*. The case in which a muscle, though still attempting to contract, is slowly letting go and lengthening is called *eccentric* or *negative work*. Do a Curl now with just your hands. Imagine the biceps shortening as you lift the hands; imagine them lowering a heavy weight and getting longer even while maintaining some contracting force.

We all know the value of positive, or concentric, work in strength training. Obviously, lifting weights makes you stronger. But how about lowering weights? This is a hot topic of debate, but with the exception of the companies whose equipment cannot let you even do negative work, most people believe in and use negative training. Negatives can be performed in many ways, as you saw earlier. In the meantime you are going to be emphasizing the negative or lowering phase of every Nautilus rep you do.

For physiological and biomechanical reasons, muscles can lower a great deal more weight than they can raise. The figure is usually in the 30–40 percent range, meaning that if you curl a 40-pound barbell, you can control the lowering of a 50- to 55-pound barbell.

This has many implications. First, to stress this extra ability during the lowering phase of each Nautilus rep, you'll have to move at about half your lifting speed. By moving more slowly, you "fool" the muscle into seeing the weight as heavier than it really is. As you've seen, you can learn how to use a friend to add resistance to the lowering phase.

Preloading Versus Afterloading

One of the goals we're trying to achieve is full range training of the muscle. If the elbow flexors can move the arm through 150-degrees of rotation, you must train them through the entire 150-degrees. Not all types of strength equipment can do this.

The technical phrase you have to understand here is *preloading versus afterloading*. A preloaded device offers you resistance right from the beginning of the movement and, if applied correctly, even stretches you into a better starting position than otherwise possible. Again use the Nautilus Pullover machine as an example. The resistance pulls the lats back into a preloaded starting position. They are now resisted at the instant contraction begins.

Afterloaded devices, such as several types of isokinetic machines, sense your input and feed it back to you. Give them one ounce of force and they resist with about an ounce. Give them 300 pounds and they give it back. Only one of several problems with these devices is that they cannot place you in a loaded, prestretched position. Full-range training is less possible, if not impossible.

Loading at Full Contraction

The second part of full-range loading is what happens at the end of the movement. Afterloaded devices give you zero when you give them zero. Imagine the end of a Biceps Curl on an afterloaded device, with your hands just sitting at your shoulders. Keep them there with an ounce of force or two, and that's all you get. With a Nautilus machine (and other preloading devices), however, your biceps are overloaded right up to and including the final position. This is full-range loading of the muscle. If the machine is further designed to prevent you from locking a joint, allowing the joint to bear the load rather than the muscles, so much the better. Score another point for Nautilus.

Unlimited Speed of Movement

The isokinetic, afterloaded devices mentioned above have another unusual feature: they limit you to movement at or below a specific speed. Set a unit at 90-degrees per second, and no matter how much force you create, you cannot move faster than 90-degrees per second. While there are some definite advantages to this concept, it may not be the best way to do strength training.

Human motion, whether at home or on the athletic field, is a series of accelerations and decelerations. It is never isokinetic, where velocity is constant and the external world changes as you change. While we're far from knowing all the answers about strength training, most experts feel that minimal accelerations and decelerations must be present to retain some similarity to real life. While you should perform at a fairly constant velocity through most of the range of movement in an exercise, maximal training gains require that you give that little extra here and there to get out the last few reps.

The Preexhaustion Principle

Most experts believe that muscles are best trained in isolation. That is, to get the most out of a muscle, you should create an exercise that focuses on it to the exclusion of others. Several Nautilus machines offer two different exercises in one frame that go beyond isolation.

There are programmed limits on the forces that your muscles can create, and you can only rarely exceed them. In the search for highest training efficiency, Nautilus Compound machines first work a muscle in isolation, then give you a second exercise that brings in other muscles to help that first one go beyond normal failure.

The combination Pullover/Torso-Arm unit is a good example. As we noted above, the resistance is applied to the lats through the elbows. When the lats reach momentary muscular failure you immediately switch to the second movement. This Torso-Arm, or Pulldown, exercise works both the lats and the rested elbow flexors. Since the biceps and brachialis did not contribute to the Pullover movement, they can help the lats tough out a few additional contractions. The concept is called *preexhaustion*, i.e., the lats are preexhausted with the first movement, then pushed even further by the second.

Here's a rundown on the Nautilus machines that offer preexhaustion:

Machine	*Order of Exercises*
Compound Leg	Leg Extension, then Leg Press
Pullover/Torso-Arm	Pullover, then Torso-Arm
Behind-Neck/Torso-Arm	Behind Neck, then Torso-Arm
Double Shoulder	Lateral Raise, then Overhead Press
Double Chest	Arm Cross, then Incline Press

CHAPTER 13

ENERGY AND MUSCLE

In explaining any complex system, you have to choose some place to start. If we were talking about cars, we might seize upon the fact that it is gasoline, exploded by the spark plugs, that provides the energy for eventual motion. So it is with the human body, with the fuel being fats, carbohydrates, and proteins. And their common denominator is our starting point: ATP.

ADENOSINE TRIPHOSPHATE—THE ULTIMATE FUEL

The basic compound whose breakdown provides the energy for all human processes, from thought to motion, is adenosine triphosphate, or ATP. Breaking off one phosphate, which leaves us with adenosine diphosphate, also releases

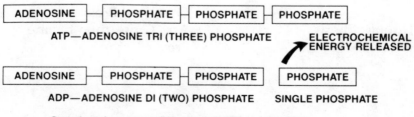

ATP—ADENOSINE TRI (THREE) PHOSPHATE

ELECTROCHEMICAL ENERGY RELEASED

ADP—ADENOSINE DI (TWO) PHOSPHATE   SINGLE PHOSPHATE

One phosphate group is broken off ATP to form ADP.
In the process, energy is released.

170

usable energy. In unique ways, organs as different as brain and muscle use this energy to function.

Where does ATP come from? It is built or synthesized by adding a loose phosphate back to an adenosine diphosphate. Sounds simple, but, you ask, where does the energy for *that* come from? Smart question. Answer: it comes from the breakdown of carbohydrates, fats, and proteins.

THE THREE ENERGY SYSTEMS

Unfortunately, the story is a bit more complicated than it appears from the above description. There are two basic systems in the body that process foodstuffs to build ATP: the anaerobic system and the aerobic system. Since the muscles maintain a store of already-built ATP and another compound called *creatine phosphate* (CP; see below), some scientists consider there to be *three* energy systems. This last one is often called the *stored phosphagens*. (Recognize the *phosphate* in there?) Here are the three energy systems in more detail:

The Stored Phosphagens

The muscles maintain enough fuel for up to 10 seconds of intense activity. In other words, a quick burst of movement requires neither anaerobic nor aerobic processing. Creatine phosphate is a neat little compound that can quickly split and release enough energy to put an ATP together from an ADP and a loose phosphate. Again, stored ATP and CP can hold you for about 10 seconds.

The Anaerobic System

Anaerobic means *without oxygen*. This system can turn on rapidly and will bear the full burden of the muscle's ATP needs for anywhere from 45 seconds to two minutes, depending on your training state. A 30-second sprint, then, will rely first on the stored phosphagens, then on the anaerobic system.

This system can work on only one type of food source: glucose. That glucose can come from either the bloodstream or the breakdown of glycogen, which is glucose stored in chains. Glycogen is found primarily in the liver and the muscles. The process of breaking down one glucose molecule results in the formation of two ATP molecules.

The anaerobic system's high speed is due to the fact that its enzymes need no warm-up time, unlike those of the aerobic system. However, what this system has in speed it lacks in endurance. What's more, its operation can result in a waste product known as *lactic acid.* Unless conditions are right, lactic acid builds up and puts a halt (and a painful one) to muscular function. The presence of the right conditions allows the aerobic system to take over.

The Aerobic System

The compound created by the anaerobic system just *before* lactic acid is called *pyruvate.* If the particular muscle being used has been working for at least $1\frac{1}{2}$–2 minutes, the aerobic enzymes have been cranked up. If sufficient oxygen can then be brought to the muscle cells by the bloodstream, pyruvate can be grabbed and processed aerobically. Voila! No lactic acid! And another 36 ATPs are created from what's left of the single, original glucose molecule!

Let's restate this important point: if we start with one glucose molecule and end at lactic acid, we get only 2 ATP molecules. If we've brought the aerobic system into play, pyruvate can give us another 36 ATP molecules. The only kicker: the aerobic system is slow. Ask for too many ATPs too fast and your body immediately resorts to the anaerobic system. This is what happens when a runner, who has been cruising along happily at a steady state, aerobic pace, starts her sprint. If she is already near her aerobic maximum, she *must* call up the anaerobic system—*and* its lactic acid, *and* fatigue. Ouch.

Before we go too far it should be added that fats and proteins can be burned only aerobically. This has great bearing on exercise for weight control. In fact, fat doesn't become

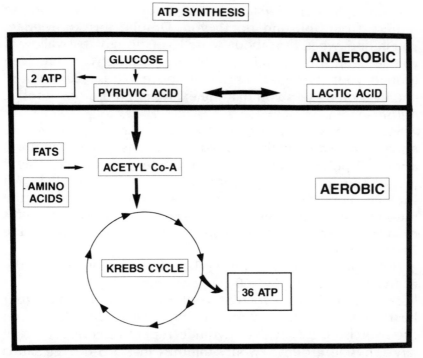

A total of 38 ATPs, along with water and carbon dioxide, are created when one glucose molecule is completely broken down. Fats and proteins (amino acids) may be burned only in the aerobic system.

the *primary* fuel for muscle until you've been working aerobically for about 30 minutes! Proteins, not meant to be used as fuel in the first place, can provide only about 15 percent of the muscle's energy needs.

Summary—The Three Energy Systems
0–10 seconds: The Stored Phosphagens
10 seconds to 2 minutes: Anaerobic System
2 minutes to ??: Aerobic System
When ATP needs exceed aerobic capacity:
Anaerobic *Plus* Aerobic

Is Nautilus Aerobic?

All that background information had a purpose—to teach

you enough to understand what various forms of exercise require from you and do to you. Despite this knowledge, you'll find what I'm about to tell you tough to swallow if you've been through a high-intensity Nautilus workout. Even though your pulse was probably above 170 for 20 minutes, and everybody tells you that the exercise is therefore aerobic, *it just isn't.*

Several labs have proven this fact. Nautilus, as well as equipment made by three other companies, at a maximum is about 60 percent aerobic and 40 percent anaerobic. This is just at the threshold for aerobic training effects. Highly fit subjects tended to be working even more anaerobically; the ratio was often reversed from 60/40 to 40/60. The full benefits of aerobic exercise don't come into play until you reach the 70–85 percent zone.

How can your heart rate be 170+ for 20 minutes with the exercise being only 40–60 percent aerobic? Shouldn't your heart rate be in your training zone for 20 minutes? Yes, your heart rate should be in your training zone for 20 minutes, but the exercise *must* involve rhythmic/repetitive contractions of large muscle groups. Twenty minutes in a 205-degree sauna will elevate many people's heart rate into the training zone, but it's not aerobic. What Nautilus machines, and other forms of high-intensity strength training, do is stress a muscle group for less than two minutes at a time, which means *anaerobically.* You then move to the next machine, and a brand-new muscle works anaerobically for the next two minutes. By the time your workout is over you've trained 10 or so major muscle groups far more anaerobically than aerobically. Few, if any, of the muscles are working rhythmically and repetitively for the 20 minutes or even for three or four minutes.

There's nothing wrong with 20 minutes of anaerobic training. You'll see loads of benefits. But don't expect to see very many aerobic benefits. You're not going to metabolize fat—glycogen is going to be the major fuel source. You won't see changes in high-density lipoproteins, the protective form of cholesterol.

Total body conditioning and preventive health care require regular aerobic exercise as a supplement to Nautilus training.

Everything you always wanted to know about aerobic exercise has been carefully fitted into Chapter 9.

A MUSCLE PRIMER: STRUCTURE, FUNCTION, AND CONTROL

Understanding something about muscle will help guide you through the maze of conflicting claims and advice. Let's start with basic structure.

Sliding Filament Theory

Muscle is composed of more than 70 percent water. About 22 percent is accounted for by two proteins: a thin strand known as *actin* and a thick one known as *myosin*. Myosin possesses tiny protein crossbridges that extend out toward the actin strands. These latter filaments are anchored in Z-disks. Given the release of calcium and the presence of magnesium, the crossbridges extend, grab, and pull the actin–Z-disk units inward. This was named the "sliding filament theory" by its discoverers A.F. and H.E. Huxley more than 20 years ago. And that's almost all there is to it.

ATP plays a strange role in this show. It *doesn't* provide the energy for contraction. When the brain fires a message off to the muscle it is the release of calcium that triggers an automatic and brief contraction. It is the breakdown of ATP to ADP, and the release of energy, that lets the crossbridges unhook and recycle for the next tiny contraction. Very strange, indeed. About eight out of 10 college physiology textbooks don't even get this deep. If anybody asks you, then, about ATP and muscle contraction, you'd almost be accurate in telling them that it makes muscle relax, not contract!

The Four Fiber Types

Four different types of skeletal muscle can be clearly identified in humans. (You probably know that there are three general categories of muscle: skeletal, cardiac, and smooth.) While the terms *fast twitch* and *slow twitch* have been popularized, there's a great deal more to the story.

Three of the four fiber types are characterized as fast and one as slow. (The three naming systems are shown in the table.) Type I, or slow fibers, are heavily aerobic—they're the ones that propel marathon runners for hours at a time. The type IIb fibers are at the other extreme—highly anaerobic and powerful but without any endurance ability. Between the I and IIb fibers lie the IIa and IIab types, which are faster than the Is but have better endurance than the IIb fibers.

THREE CLASSIFICATION SCHEMES

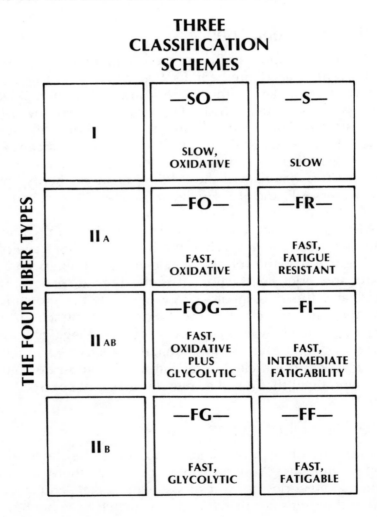

THE FOUR FIBER TYPES

I	**—SO—** SLOW, OXIDATIVE	**—S—** SLOW
II A	**—FO—** FAST, OXIDATIVE	**—FR—** FAST, FATIGUE RESISTANT
II AB	**—FOG—** FAST, OXIDATIVE PLUS GLYCOLYTIC	**—FI—** FAST, INTERMEDIATE FATIGABILITY
II B	**—FG—** FAST, GLYCOLYTIC	**—FF—** FAST, FATIGABLE

Generally speaking, the quadriceps of world class sprinters are usually very high in IIb fibers, while marathoners show a predominance of type Is. There are so many factors that contribute to performance, though, that many elite marathoners show only average type I fiber percentages. This is nice, because the percentage of fibers you're born with is roughly the percentage you finish with. Training has little or no effect on the relative distribution of fast and slow fibers in a muscle. Most of us have an even mix of I, IIa, and IIb fibers. The IIab type exists but is fairly rare.

While we're on the subject of genetics, I should note that fiber types are not the only performance determinant that is genetically fixed. Such limits appear to exist on all these factors. This is no reason to quit, though, since you can improve greatly on all factors, and what you might lack in fiber type you might make up for in aerobic capacity. Some of the fastest marathons in history have been run with legs that were only 60 percent slow-twitch muscle. There's hope for us all!

How It Grows

Believe it or not, no one on earth yet knows exactly what makes muscle grow. Intensity obviously plays a role, but the actual mechanism remains somewhat a mystery. The most popular theory states that intense contractions actually tear actin proteins out of their Z-disks. The muscle appears to respond to this by rebuilding to a stronger and larger state.

On the subject of things we don't know, we also are pretty much in the dark as to exactly why women show the same percentage strength gains as men without the same increases in size. The most plausible theory is that women learn to recruit muscle more efficiently, a case of making better use of what they have. Whatever the reason, most women will gain all the strength they want or need without the sometimes visually displeasing size gains. This is discussed in more detail in Chapter 11.

We do know, however, the factors that explain the increase

in size of a muscle, known as *hypertrophy*. There are four causes:

- actual increase in muscle proteins
- increase in the strength and quantity of connective tissue running through the muscle
- increase in the number of myofibrils, the tiny actin-plus-myosin cables within one muscle fiber
- increase in the number of blood capillaries running through the muscle

There has been considerable debate over the occurrence of a phenomenon known as *hyperplasia,* an increase in the number of muscle fibers. At this time it appears that fibers may reach a maximum size, then split if trained further. The book isn't closed, though.

How It's All Controlled

It's a word you've heard before, and it has the same meaning as when Uncle Sam mutters it—*recruitment*. The term refers to that process through which the brain selects and controls muscle. Contrary to about 92 percent of what you will hear (usually from a coach who has never taken any neuroscience courses), the brain recruits muscle in an orderly fashion.

Most of you will hear the terms *fast twitch* and *slow twitch* and conclude that fast movements use fast muscle, and slow movements use slow muscle. Wrong. Bad choice of names for the fibers, I've always said, for that's *not* how the brain works.

Regardless of the task, the brain appears always to call on the type I or slow fibers first. The brain is essentially a lazy organ, and since the type I fibers are the easiest to turn on electrically, the first bit of output from brain to muscle turns them on.

The world's confusion results from the slow fibers being slow only *in comparison to* the fast fibers. They are capable of creating *very* fast movements if they don't have a heavy load to move. That's where those coaches go wrong. They assume that fast training will cause the brain to use the fast fibers, without realizing that unless the load is heavy, the slow, type I fibers will suffice.

I always use the analogy of my relatively fast German car, which becomes slow in comparison to a friend's very expensive German sports car. Think of slow-twitch muscle as weak muscle. If you need to move a very light load very fast, slow-twitch muscle will do the job. Don't think of it as slow muscle.

In order for the brain to call on or recruit the IIb fibers, it must be shown that a great deal of force is needed. Here's where the orderly recruitment comes in. Remember that the brain is lazy—for it first adds in the IIa fibers if the type Is can't create enough force to move the heavy load at desired speed. If these aren't enough, it adds the IIab fibers. Only if the I, IIa, *and* IIab fibers can't do the job will the brain be forced to recruit the IIbs. Recruitment order follows the ranking of fibers from easiest to turn on (type I) to hardest (type IIb).

If you go into strength training with the goal of moving a weight quickly, you will obviously be forced to use light loads. The heavier the load, the slower the maximal speed, and that's a law of physics. As you try to increase the speed, you must lighten the load you're lifting. And the lighter the load, the less chance the brain will be forced to recruit the IIb fibers. But get out onto the field or into the pool and try to move your 125-pound body quickly, and you'll find you need those IIbs. It would be too bad, wouldn't it, if you'd never trained them in the weight room!

Nautilus, and in fact all strength training, should be approached only as a method to train the IIb fibers quickly so that they can be applied in *perfectly skill-specific ways* on the athletic field. Yes, sprinters must run fast in training. Yes, swimmers must swim fast in training. But to get the maximum benefits from strength work, slow speed and high intensity are the keys.

INDEX